BEFORE THE AIRCRAFT CARRIER

BEFORE THE AIRCRAFT CARRIER

The Development of Aviation Vessels 1849-1922

R D Layman

Foreword by the late Rear Admiral George van Deurs, US Navy retired

Naval
Institute
Press

For Boris V Drashpil (1902–87), mentor, colleague, friend

First published in Great Britain 1989 by
Conway Maritime Press Limited
24 Bride Lane, Fleet Street
London EC4Y 8DR

Published and distributed in the United States of
America and Canada by the Naval Institute Press
Annapolis, Maryland 21402

Library of Congress Catalog Card No
89-60444

ISBN 0-87021-210-9

Manufactured in Great Britain

Contents

Foreword

FOR MANY CENTURIES, seamen climbed to mastheads to increase their range of vision. Especially if they believed danger to be near, many of them must have wished that their lookouts could ride even higher – with the sea birds. When a gull splotched an upturned face, men's thoughts probably turned to similarly smacking an enemy with something harder. Hence, as soon as balloons lifted men, navies tried to take them to sea. During the American Civil War, they tried captive balloons tied to boats. In 1911, Glenn Curtiss built his first successful float plane hoping to sell it to the navy for development.

Before World War I ended, in 1918, most navies had used aircraft and balloons on their regular war vessels. In addition, at least nine countries fitted out special ships as aircraft (that is seaplane) carriers. These vessels were tried worldwide, from the North Sea and the Baltic to the Red Sea and the South Indian Ocean, from the Caspian Sea to the North Atlantic and the Gulf of Mexico. Great Britain fitted out the greatest number, in her desperate effort to intercept German airships attacking over the North Sea. She tried all types of vessels from blue ribbon transatlantic liners to submarines but none of them had much effect on the outcome of that war.

This book ends in the early 1920s, when the development of aircraft vessels split to follow three separate trails through World War II. Interest was concentrated on the flight-deck carrier type as soon as their operation began. The spectacular and rapid development of this new type pushed interest in seaplane carriers into the background, and these wartime pioneers were almost entirely forgotten, as the men who had sailed them died.

Large seaplanes supported by tenders (not carriers) served navies well for at least a decade after World War II. Some of these flying boats were larger than many of the World War I 'airplane carriers'.

The third development between the world wars consisted of small seaplanes carried by combatant ships for spotting gunfire and scouting. No one ever considered classifying the ships they served as 'aircraft carriers'.

In this book R D Layman, a newspaperman with a lifelong interest in all phases of seagoing aviation, has collected the almost-forgotten stories of the ships that first specialized in naval aviation. His book should be of special interest to aviators, historians, and everyone who takes pride in today's great aircraft carriers. For anyone interested in the origins of today's super carriers, it is essential reading.

George van Deurs
Rear Admiral, US Navy, retired

Preface

THIS BOOK DESCRIBES, with particulars and brief histories, the surface craft that, over a span of seventy-three years, were employed experimentally or operationally in attempts to adapt aerial devices to the service of naval warfare. Many of these were influential in the development of shipboard aviation; others were less so but are included because of their inherent interest.

The World War I vessels listed are those employed solely or principally for aeronautical purposes; no attempt has been made to list the many hundreds of other ships that carried aircraft or balloons during 1914–18, although a few are noted briefly.

Particulars of ships used in aviation experiments after the introduction of the aeroplane, but which did not become permanent aviation vessels, are omitted, as they are considered irrelevant to those experiments; their details may be found in the Conway Fighting Ships series.

Although, as the title indicates, the book is devoted largely to vessels predating the flight-deck carrier, the purview has been extended to cover the first three such ships because they represent the culmination of more than a half century of theory, experiment and practical experience.

I am indebted to scores of individuals and more than a dozen institutions for invaluable assistance in making this book possible. To single out some for special acknowledgment would be to slight the others; to cite all, and their special contributions, would require many pages. I can but extend my most sincere and humble thanks to all those who over thirty years have provided assistance, from Australia, Austria, Belgium, Canada, Czechoslovakia, France, Italy, Japan, Malta, The Netherlands, New Zealand, Poland, South Africa, the Soviet Union, Spain, Sweden, Switzerland, the United Kingdom, the United States and West Germany.

Above all, I am grateful to my wife, Marget Murray Layman, for support, encouragement, long-suffering patience, wise advice and skilful editing.

Introduction

'FANCY... WHEN IN SOME great conflict of the future a splendid up-to-date battleship fleet of the traditional order... finds itself beset in midseas by a couple of great, unarmored, liner-like hulls, engined to admit of speeds and steaming radii such as will permit them to pursue or run away from any armored craft yet built, and designed with clear and level decks for aeroplane launching. Conceive them provided with storage room for hundreds of... aeroplanes, with fuel, repair facilities, and explosives, and with housing for a regiment or two of expert air navigators. Then picture the terribly one-sided engagement that will ensue — the thousands of tons and millions of dollars' worth of cunningly-fashioned mechanism all but impotent against the unremitted, harrying, and reinforced attacks from aloft, and unable either to escape from or give chase to the enemy's floating bases of supplies, which, ever warned and convoyed by their aerial supports, will unreachably maneuver out of gun range... reprovisioning, remanning, launching and relaunching their winged messengers of death until the cold waters close over the costly armada of some nation that has refused to profit by the lessons of progress.'

So wrote Victor Loughheed, in 1909, in a purple passage that might have described an aeronaval engagement of World War II. He was the half-brother of Malcolm and Allan Loughhead, founders of what is now the Lockheed Corporation. The full brothers eventually changed the spelling of the family name to conform with its pronounciation; Victor, who did not pursue an aeronautical career after 1910, had earlier adopted a compromise spelling. Victor Loughheed was not the first nor the last to predict the aircraft carrier.

About the same time or earlier, French aeronautical pioneer Clément Ader, who some French aero scholars persist in maintaining achieved powered flight before the Wright brothers, gave a remarkably clear forecast, writing of a ship whose upper deck 'will have to be cleared of any obstacles. It will be flat, as wide as possible, not conforming to the lines of the hull... Servicing the aircraft will have to be done below this deck... Access to this lower deck will be by means of a lift long enough and wide enough to take an aircraft with its wings folded. Along the sides will be the workshops of the mechanics... The speed of this vessel will have to be at least as great as that of cruisers...' The loosely translated passage has been cited as from the 1895 edition of his book *L'aviation militaire* but it is more likely to be from a later edition.

Many others, both aviators and naval officers or administrators, envisioned much the same thing, logic impelling them to the same elementary conclusion that if aircraft with wheels were to function from a ship, that ship must have a long, flat, unobstructed area for takeoff and landing. By the fateful year 1914, the aircraft carrier was an idea whose time had come.

Dreams of employing aerial devices in war at sea had long antedated the concept of the aircraft carrier, inspiring visionaries or theorists centuries before any form of human flight had been achieved. The dream became a realistic possibility with the advent of the balloon in the late eighteenth century, but it was not until 1849–62 that that craft was used in maritime conflict. During much of the rest of the nineteenth century and into the early years of the twentieth, many navies experimented with balloons lofted from and towed by ships – not for the offensive purpose for which they had first been employed, but for observation, which included, in the later years, the detection of submarines and mines. Around the turn of the century, shipboard use of the man-lifting kite was also investigated.

The balloon observer had a far wider field of vision than the man in the crow's nest, but even his was still limited. With the introduction of the airship and the aeroplane, which possessed the independent mobility the balloon and kite lacked, the limits of aerial scouting at sea were hugely expanded, and it was for that reason that these craft attracted naval interest at an early stage of their development. Their employment as offensive weapons, although advocated and predicted frequently and enthusiastically, was yet to be proved feasible. So, by the start of World War I, the airship and the aeroplane had eclipsed the balloon as naval aerial scouts, although the balloon would be re-introduced into naval service during that conflict and would reach its maritime apogee by 1918.

At first, the seaplane appeared to be the ideal shipboard craft. It was assumed that it could be easily carried by a warship, and the waters of the entire world were open to its use. The seaplane, however, had inherent handicaps. It was at the mercy of the state of the water from which it operated and its performance in the air was hampered by the very features that enabled it to function from water. This was especially true of the floatplane. The flying boat could be made quite seaworthy, but only by an increase in size that made its shipboard carriage impractical. Despite these disadvantages, the seaplane was sufficiently useful for it to remain in naval service for decades. By the end of the period covered by this book, it still played an important part in naval aviation. The catapult had been developed as a more reliable and faster way of getting it into the air than lowering it over the side.

With the exception of three balloon-carrying craft, described later in these pages, the specialized aviation vessel did not exist except on paper until nearly the eve of World War I. France, in 1912, was the first nation to modify a warship significantly and permanently for aeronautical service. Britain, in 1914, was the first to build an ocean-going, self-propelled vessel for that purpose; thereafter, she became the world leader in shipboard aviation.

A significant influence was Britain's need to defend itself against the German rigid airship, perfected in the early years of the century by Count Ferdinand von Zeppelin. At the start of the war the airship menace was largely imaginary, but it soon became real. The Zeppelin threat was twofold: as a far-ranging scout able to detect British fleet movements and as a bomber spewing destruction on British cities. Countering this threat meant attacking it either in the air or at its bases. Both methods demanded that aircraft be carried on ships, for at sea the airships were targets of opportunity, and their bases were beyond the range of land-based aircraft.

The seaplane proved unsuitable for either form of attack because of its total dependence on favourable seas. The need was for aircraft that could take off directly from ships. Thus the British aviation vessel evolved from a simple seaplane carrier to a ship that could launch wheeled aircraft but not recover them, to a craft able both to launch and recover. Other countries, free of the difficulties posed for Britain by the North Sea, could skip the intermediate stage.

Aircraft were not taken to sea in World War I solely for their anti-airship role; their original naval role of reconnaissance remained important. Outside the North Sea, the Royal Navy, as well as others that did not have to confront the airship, found shipboard aviation valuable in many respects. Off the coasts of the Levant, Arabia, Africa, Courland, Anatolia, Bulgaria and China, the seaplane carrier and the balloon ship provided useful and sometimes decisive air support to forces that would otherwise have lacked it.

Moreover, by 1917 technical advances in aircraft had begun to give them the offensive power that had been predicted before 1914. This power opened new horizons in naval thought. The different attitudes to shipboard aviation of two successive commanders of the Grand Fleet is an instructive example. Whereas, in 1915, Admiral Sir John Jellicoe, who might be described as less air-minded than air-obsessed, appealed for an airplane-carrying ship or two to drive away the Zeppelins, the highly air-minded Admiral Sir David Beatty, in 1918, called for entire divisions of carriers to attack the German fleet at its bases.

The aircraft carrier had been conceived in fertile minds by 1914, and its appearance was inevitable, but the exigencies of World War I initiated the gestation earlier than might otherwise have been the case. The progress to birth was remarkably swift, in view of the labour involved, for what seemed so simple in the imagination was not easy to translate into reality. Creation of the flight-deck carrier presented a host of problems hitherto unknown in the history of steamship design. Their solution by mainly unsung naval architects, of whom Britain's were in the vanguard, would bestow upon seapower a greater versatility and strength than it had ever before possessed. The vessel that was produced became the ultimate arbiter of maritime conflict during World War II, and perhaps remains so today.

Austria/Austria-Hungary

To the navy of Austria (Austria-Hungary after establishment of the Dual Monarchy in 1867) goes credit for the first-known offensive use of aerial devices by a warship.

Austrian sidewheel steamer *Vulcano*, first vessel to employ aerial weapons offensively. *Courtesy of Anthony Sokol*

VULCANO

Tonnage:	483t
Dimensions:	157f 9int × 25ft × ? (48m × 7.6m × ?)
Machinery:	steam engine, 2 sidewheel paddles, 120ihp = ?
Armament:	2–28pdr, 2–12pdr
Complement:	93

No other particulars known

Built in Venice in 1842–44, *Vulcano* was one of the Austrian navy's earliest steamships. In 1848–49 she was one of the units blockading Venice during the Austrian siege of that city.

In an attempt to reach targets beyond the range of their artillery, the besiegers bombarded the city by means of hot-air balloons launched when winds were favourable and carrying explosive charges calibrated to drop at various times. On 12 July 1849, an unknown number of these balloons was launched from the deck of *Vulcano*. The attempt was unsuccessful, contrary winds blowing them back over the ship, and the experiment was not repeated.

Vulcano was later renamed *Vulcan* and remained in service until 1872, when she was reduced to a hulk. She was stricken to become a coal hulk in 1882 and her final fate seems to be unknown.

The only other known operation of a balloon by the Austrian navy occurred on 10 June 1912, when the submarine *U5* towed a kite balloon in what was apparently an experiment to determine the best coloration for submarines to avoid detection underwater.

The creation of an air arm for the Kaiserlich und Königlich (Imperial and Royal) Navy began in 1909 with the dispatch of a few officers to flight training abroad. An experimental naval air station was set up at Pola in 1911 and a formal naval air branch was established before the outbreak of war in 1914.

Although small in comparison with those of other powers, the K u K air arm performed excellently during the war. Equipped almost entirely with flying boats of splendid quality, it established air superiority over the Adriatic until overwhelmed numerically after 1916.

Because of the short range of Adriatic air operations, especially in its northern reaches, plus the many harbours, coves, bays and inlets along its long Austrian coastline which provided fine sheltered waters for seaplanes, the K u K navy had no need for aviation vessels. It did, however, open the war with shipboard transport of aircraft. On 22 July 1914, the battleships *Erzerzog Franz Ferdinand*, *Radetzky* and *Zrinyi* each carried a flying boat from Pola to the Gulf of Cattaro, from which the next day they reconnoitered the Montenegrin border in the war's first operational flights by naval planes. (Battleships had performed the same service in April 1913, taking flying boats to Cattaro as part of an international peacekeeping force during the troubled period of the Balkan Wars.)

Later in the war, the old coastal torpedo boat *No 14* (ex-*Kigyo*) served as a seaplane tender, transporting flying boats occasionally, and the naval yacht *Taurus* was an accommodation ship for naval aircrew at Pola.

Confederate States of America

The American Civil War saw the first use of balloons in naval warfare, although they were restricted to riverine operations. The Union Navy employed waterborne balloons on several occasions, to be noted later, but the Confederacy tried the technique only once, with an unfortunate conclusion.

TEASER

Tonnage:	64t (65.03 tonnes)
Dimensions:	80ft × 18ft × 7ft
	(24.5m × 7.48m × 2.13m)
Machinery:	steam engine, 1 shaft
Armament:	1–32pdr, 1–12pdr

An artist's depiction of the Confederate balloon boat *Teaser* just before her capture on 4 July 1862. The rendering may be inaccurate. *Naval History Division*

This single-screw steamship was built as a tug in Philadelphia, probably in 1855, although the date is not definitely known, and may have originally been named *Wide Awake*. She was purchased at Richmond, Virginia, in early 1861 for service with the Virginia State Navy and was renamed *Teaser* either then or upon her incorporation into the Confederate States Navy when that service was formed after Virginia's secession from the Union on 17 April 1861.

Teaser served as a tender to the Confederate iron-clad *Virginia* (ex-USS *Merrimack*) during her engagements with Union vessels, including USS *Monitor*, 8–9 March 1862. In June 1862, she was assigned to lay torpedoes (mines) in the James River, and, later that month, chosen as the vessel to embark a balloon for waterborne reconnaissance of Union positions along the James. The spherical balloon was inflated with commercial coal gas from the Richmond municipal gas works, conveniently located on the banks of the river. It has gone into legend as the 'silk dress balloon' supposedly manufactured from gowns donated by patriotic Southern belles. In fact, it had been manufactured from raw silk, early in 1862 at Savannah, Georgia, and had seen service earlier in the Peninsula campaign, sometimes towed by a railway locomotive.

Teaser operated the balloon from 1–3 July with unknown results. On 4 July she was engaged and captured with the balloon aboard by the Union sidewheel gunboat *Maratanza*, given distant support by USS *Monitor*. She was taken into the Union Navy without change of name and was sold out of service on 24 June 1865, presumably to return to mercantile use under the name *York River* as registered on 3 July 1865. She was stricken from the US shipping registry in 1873, and her ultimate fate is unknown.

Although *Teaser*'s aeronautical service contributed nothing to the Confederate war effort, her presence, together with that of *Monitor*, in the March and June actions is an interesting coincidental link between the first clash of ironclad warships and one of the earliest uses of a waterborne aerial device.

France

Foudre in her original configuration as a torpedo boat carrier, but with an inflated spherical balloon on her quarterdeck during Mediterranean manoeuvres of 1898 or 1901. *Marius Bar*

The French navy's association with aeronautics might fancifully be said to date from 1798, when a unit of the Compagnie d'Aérostiers, the world's first organized military air arm, was embarked with at least one balloon on a ship named *Le Patriote* that was assigned to reconnoitre the Egyptian coast in advance of the Napoleonic invasion fleet. Unfortunately, she ran onto rocks and sank off Alexandria on 4 July 1798. The wreck was located in 1986 and some artifacts recovered. Some aeronautical gear may also have been aboard the line-of-battle ship *L'Orient* when she was destroyed at Aboukir. In neither case was there any thought of using balloons from shipboard; they were being transported for operations ashore.

By the start of the twentieth century, the French navy had become a considerable user of shipboard balloons and man-lifting kites (although the balloon branch was disbanded in 1904). From there, it was but a short step into heavier-than-air aviation, in which France was the world leader for a time before World War I (the very word 'aviation' itself being a French coinage).

Much interest was shown in taking aircraft to sea on ships, even before a naval air arm, the Service Aéronautique, was officially established in 1912. Already one vessel, *Foudre* (qv), had been modified to carry aircraft, and in May 1912 investigation of a flight-deck ship was recommended. Several plans were advanced, and, by the end of the year, at least semi-official authorization had been given for construction of such a ship. Until it was completed, another ship, the British tanker *Fornebo*, was considered for purchase and conversion to replace *Foudre*, which was originally regarded as no more than an experimental stop-gap. *Fornebo* resembled the British seaplane carrier *Ark Royal* (qv) after that vessel's redesign, leading one to think that French naval architects had arrived independently, and perhaps earlier, at a similar configuration for an aviation vessel, that is, machinery and main superstructure right aft.

Few details of what was to have been the special ship have survived, and it is unclear whether it was to have been entirely or only partially a flight-deck vessel. It

The aircraft hangar installed on *Foudre* in 1912, the first aboard a warship. The aircraft is a Voisin, the French navy's first floatplane. *Boris V Drashpil collection*

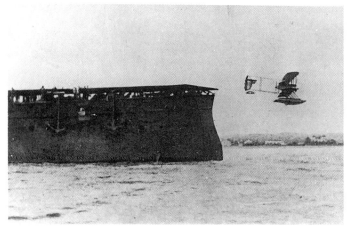

The Caudron G.III amphibian flown by René Caudron taking off from *Foudre*'s platform, 8 May 1914 – the first aircraft takeoff from a French vessel. *Musée de l'Air*

Foudre in her final guise as a seaplane carrier. The hangar is retained but the takeoff platform has been replaced by a seaplane-handling platform. *Marius Bar*

was, however, apparently to have had an armoured hangar, the first suggestion of that feature for an aviation vessel.

On the eve of World War I, plans were under way for development of catapults to equip cruisers and battleships, and also for a system of launching and recovering aircraft on wires, an idea that had been successfully tested on land. There was also an ambitious naval airship programme which was still on paper.

All these schemes were halted by the war, at first in the expectation of a short conflict and later because of the heavy demands upon French industry for *matériel* for the land fronts and for France's allies. In fact, all French naval shipbuilding above the level of destroyer was suspended for the duration of the war.

French naval aviation, which went to war with only a handful of seaplanes, advanced greatly in both quantity and quality during the conflict – especially after 1916 when it was needed to combat the U-boat menace – but its shipboard aspects went into abeyance. Plans for the special aviation vessel languished on the drawing board until they vanished into limbo about 1917. It was not until the early 1920s that experiments with shipboard launching of aircraft were resumed, special shipboard aircraft were designed and the first flight-deck carrier, built on the hull of the incomplete battleship *Normandie*, was authorized.

FOUDRE

Displacement:	5971t normal, 6089t full load
Dimensions:	390ft 4in × 66ft 2in × 17ft 6in normal, 23ft 6in full load
	(118.7m × 17.2m × 5.4m, 7.20m)
Machinery:	2 sets triple expansion, 24 boilers, 2 shafts, 11,800ihp = 19.6kts 7500nm at 10kts, 1395 nm at 19kts. Coal 798t (926 tonnes)
Armour:	4.2in (105.40mm) deck, 3.9in (100mm) conning tower, 2.1in (54mm) casemates
Armament:	8–3.9in/45 (100mm) 8 × 1; 4–65mm/50 4 × 1; 4–47mm/50 4 × 1 (some 100mm later replaced by army 90mm)
Aircraft arrangements:	45ft 11in (13.74m) × 29ft 6in (9m) × 13ft 1in (3.99m) hangar; 114ft (34.70m) × 26ft (8m) launching platform fitted forward in 1914, later replaced by seaplane handling platform; 4 to 8 aircraft
Complement:	431 originally

Name	Builder	Laid down	Launched	Completed	Fate
FOUDRE	Ateliers et Chantiers de La Gironde, Bordeaux	6.9.1892	20.10.1895	1896	BU 1922

This vessel, whose name was changed from *Seine* during construction, was conceived in 1890 at the height of the Jeune École as a carrier for eight small torpedo boats. With the demise of that doctrine, she spent much of her early career transporting torpedo boats and submarines to colonial ports. She was converted to a repair ship in 1907 and in 1910 was fitted for minelaying.

Foudre's first association with aeronautics came when she operated a spherical balloon experimentally during Mediterranean manoeuvres in 1898 and 1901. With the beginnings of French naval aviation in 1911, she was selected as a general-purpose aircraft test-bed vessel, largely because her extensive repair facilities could handle airframes and aero engines.

Foudre was modified for this role at Toulon. The work, completed in March 1912, consisted mainly of installation of an aircraft hangar – the first ever fitted

in a warship – aft of her third funnel. Her first aircraft, a Voisin floatplane, was embarked 27 May 1912 and she operated this aircraft and others in pre-World War I manoeuvres.

To test the feasibility of shipboard takeoff, a platform was installed over her forecastle by Ingénieurs des Chantiers et Ateliers de Provence at Port-de-Bouc in early 1914. From it, the civilian pilot and aeronautical designer René Caudron made the first French shipboard takeoff on 8 May 1914 in a Caudron G.III amphibian floatplane of his own design. A second attempt on 9 June by one of the first French naval aviators, Lieutenant de Vaisseau (later Admiral) Jean de Laborde, ended in a crash. The platform was subsequently removed, but replaced later in 1914 by a seaplane-handling platform.

With the outbreak of war in 1914, *Foudre* was attached to the Armée Navale, the main French

A Nieuport VI under hoist by *Campinas* c1915, possibly at the Dardanelles. This twin-float, two-place, 100-hp monoplane was a mainstay of French shipboard aviation during the early war years, serving on both *Campinas* and *Foudre* as well as from shore bases until replaced by FBA flying boats. *Author's collection*

fleet in the Mediterranean, based in Malta. She was equipped with Nicuport floatplanes that had been ordered by Turkey but taken over for French service. *Foudre* accompanied the fleet on some sorties into the Adriatic in support of Montenegro, but her aircraft had no opportunity to accomplish anything of value to the fleet. Because of this apparent uselessness, she was ordered to Port Said in late 1914.

There, her aircraft, operating from British vessels with French pilots and British observers, proved their worth by providing information invaluable to the repulse of the Turkish thrust against the Suez Canal in early 1915.

Based at Mudros, *Foudre* again operated her Nieuports from 15 March to 23 May 1915 during the early stages of the Dardanelles-Gallipoli campaign but they were severely handicapped by their lack of wireless.

Foudre was dry docked at Toulon from late May to August for repair and refitting; when she returned to service, her Nieuports were replaced by FBA (Franco British Aviation) flying boats. For the rest of the war, however, *Foudre* performed little aviation duty aside from accompanying the French fleet during the Athens intervention in June 1917. During 1916–18 she became known as a seagoing *Maître Jacques*, serving as a depot and repair ship for submarines and small craft and administrative flagship for Eastern Mediterranean patrol units, based at Port Said and various Aegean ports.

After the armistice, she performed patrol duty in the Adriatic until August 1919. Placed in reserve at Toulon in 1920, she was stricken on 1 December 1921, and sold for breaking up 27 May 1922.

Although *Foudre*'s career was unspectacular, she occupies a unique place in naval history as the first warship to be permanently altered for service as an aviation vessel.

Campinas as converted to a seaplane carrier with canvas hangars fore and aft. *Marius Bar*

CAMPINAS

Displacement:	3319grt (3372 tonnes standard)
Dimensions:	357ft 6in oa × 42ft 7in × 25ft 2in mean
	(109m × 12.85m × 7.08m)
Machinery:	1 set triple expansion, 2 boilers, 1 shaft, 1460ihp = 11.5kts. Coal 988t (1000 tonnes)
Armament:	1–3.9in/45 (100mm), 1–47mm/50
Aircraft arrangements:	canvas hangars over fore and aft cargo hold wells; seaplane handling booms on foremast and mainmast. 6 to 10 aircraft
Complement:	?

Name	Builder	Laid down	Launched	Completed	Fate
CAMPINAS	Ateliers et Chantiers de La Loire, Saint Nazaire	1894	1896	1897	?

This Chargeurs Reunis cargo-liner was requisitioned in late 1915 for use as a carrier for the Port Said seaplane unit, and was converted for the role at Port Said by the Compagnie Universelle du Canal de Suez. The conversion was hasty and incomplete, consisting mainly of installation of canvas aircraft shelters fore and aft. *Campinas* may also have been equipped for operation of a kite balloon, but this is doubtful.

Her first aircraft were Nieuport floatplanes, replaced in 1916 or early 1917 by FBA flying boats.

After commissioning as a carrier in January 1916 at Port Said, she operated in the eastern Mediterranean-Aegean-Levant area for the rest of the war, also taking part in the Athens intervention in 1917. Her operations were apparently useful, but entirely undistinguished. She is believed to have been returned to her owners after the war but her subsequent history is uncertain.

A Nieuport floatplane alongside *Campinas* c1915, probably at Malta. *Author's collection*

Paddlewheel Channel packet *Nord* with aircraft hangars aft. *Pas-de-Calais* was similar in appearance.
Courtesy of Jacques Szynka

NORD, PAS-DE-CALAIS

Displacement:	1541grt (1565 tonnes)
Dimensions:	338ft 6in × 35ft × 11ft
	(102.9m × 8.9m × 3.3m)
Machinery:	reciprocating engines, 2 side paddlewheels, 7800ihp = 21kts
Armament:	2–47mm/50
Aircraft arrangements:	1 permanent hangar amidships, 1 canvas hangar aft; 2 or at times possibly 3 aircraft
Complement:	?

Name	Builder	Laid down	Launched	Completed	Fate
NORD	Ateliers et Chantiers de La Loire, Saint Nazaire	1897	1898	1899	?
PAS-DE-CALAIS		1897	1898	1899	?

These vessels are of interest mainly for their novelty as two of the only six paddlewheel aviation vessels ever to exist, the others being the British *Brocklesby* and *Killingholme* (qv) and the American *Sable* and *Wolverine* of World War II.

Nord and *Pas-de-Calais* were built in tandem as cross-Channel packets for Cie Chemins de Fer du Nord and both were requisitioned by the French navy at the outset of World War I for service as patrol vessels rated as light auxiliary cruisers. *Nord* was detached in October 1914 to serve as a hospital ship for the British Red Cross. She would, of course, have been disarmed before starting this service, and it is not clear whether either vessel was armed when they were converted to auxiliary seaplane carriers, *Pas-de-Calais* commissioning on 1 July 1915 and *Nord* on 26 June 1916. *Pas-de-Calais*, based at Cherbourg, and *Nord*, at Dunkirk, carried out what seem to have been uneventful patrols until some time in 1917, when they ceased aviation service. A proposal in 1916 to increase their aircraft capacity to four was not acted upon.

Their aircraft were FBA flying boats; a report that one or both may have, at one time, embarked a British Admiralty Type 184 Short floatplane is almost certainly incorrect.

Both vessels were returned to mercantile service in 1919, probably to their original owner, but their postwar history is unknown.

Two other vessels served at least briefly as French auxiliary seaplane carriers in World War I. *Rouen*, a 1656-ton, 24-knot Channel packet requisitioned in 1914 as an auxiliary cruiser, was equipped to carry two FBA flying boats in 1916 while undergoing repair for mine damage. She served as a convoy escort in the Mediterranean in 1917 but later was employed as a transport, at which time the aircraft undoubtedly were removed.

Dorade, a mercantile ex-German war prize that may have been a large trawler, carried an FBA flying boat for North African coastal patrol in 1917, based at Casablanca. Nothing else appears to be known about this vessel.

Postwar, the *Arras*-class sloop *Bapaume* was used as a test vessel in experiments preliminary to the redesign of the incomplete battleship *Normandie* as a flight-deck carrier renamed *Béarn*. A platform was fitted over the sloop's forecastle from which successful takeoffs were made by Nieuport single-seat fighters.

Another unit of this class, *Belfort*, served as a seaplane tender between the wars, fitted with an aircraft-handling crane aft, and armament reduced to one 3in gun.

Sloop *Bapaume* fitted with forward platform for takeoff experiments in March 1921. *Marius Bar*

Germany

Aside from a brief experiment in towing a kite balloon from a torpedo boat, the German navy had shown no discernible interest in shipboard aeronautics before World War I. This was not because of lack of interest in aviation, for efforts to create a fleet air arm had begun in 1910, but these efforts were hampered by the reluctance of the German aircraft industry to develop aircraft to the navy's initially over-rigid specifications, and, at the outbreak of war, these were a motley collection of mostly individual types, many of them foreign.

Aside from this problem, which was quickly and radically solved, aviation vessels seemed superfluous in the area in which the High Seas Fleet expected to fight – the shallows and narrows of the German North Sea coast, where the naval high command mistakenly believed the British navy would try to establish a classic nineteenth-century close blockade. Aerial support there could easily come from bases – some of which were established even before there were aircraft for them – on the mainland, the East Frisian islands and the fortress island of Heligoland. If longer-range aerial reconnaissance were needed, it could be provided by rigid airships, although their technical perfection by Count Ferdinand von Zeppelin had not been matched by service experience.

Contrary to myth, the German navy possessed only one operational Zeppelin when war came, two having been lost in prewar accidents. The rise of the Zeppelin was a wartime phenomenon in response to the High Seas Fleet's shortage of scouting cruisers, a deficiency caused by the construction policies of Grossadmiral Alfred von Tirpitz during creation of his 'risk navy'. The airships' later use in the bombing campaign against British mainland targets was another matter altogether.

Nevertheless, upon the outbreak of hostilities, naval authorities reasoned that the North Sea air bases could be usefully supplemented by seaplane-carrying ships, and two of these were authorized eight days before the Royal Navy took a similar step.

Here, one is tempted to see a contrast in national and naval temperament and policy. The British chose speedy Channel packets intended to accompany the fleet in seagoing offensive operations; the Germans selected slow vessels which although perhaps intended for fleet work could, in practice, only plod from harbour to harbour to put planes up for defensive reconnaissance. The British carriers were crudely converted in a matter of weeks and were operational almost immediately; the German vessels were far more elaborately equipped but were unfit for operations, had to go back for modifications, and did not enter service until 1915.

The unaggressive attitude of the German navy in the North Sea, where it passively awaited a British attack, was not shared by the Baltic fleet. In that sea, the navy was often on the offensive, and if aircraft were to assist it in reaches beyond the range of shore- or harbour-based machines, they would have to be carried by ship. German shipboard air operations were in fact initiated there by the commander of Baltic naval forces, Grossadmiral Prinz Heinrich of Prussia. The younger brother of Kaiser Wilhelm II, Heinrich was a qualified aviator, having learned to fly in 1910, and an influential force in the creation of the German naval air arm. It was at his directive that two seaplanes were embarked on the armoured cruiser *Friedrich Karl* in November 1914 to scout Russian ports. One was still aboard when the cruiser was sunk by a mine on 17 November.

German cruisers and destroyers subsequently embarked seaplanes several times for Baltic operations, and it was there, although infrequently, that German seaplane carriers were used as aggressively as British carriers in the North Sea.

ANSWALD (FS I)

Displacement:	5401grt (5487 tonnes)
Dimensions:	440ft × 54ft 6in × 24ft
	(133.6m × 16.6m × 7.4m)
Machinery:	2 sets compound engines, 3 boilers, 1 shaft, 2800ihp — 11kts
Armament:	2–3.4in/45 (88mm) AA
Aircraft arrangements:	forward hangar 54ft (16.4m) × 40ft 8in (12.4m), aft hangar 55ft 6in (16.9m) × 39ft (12m); 2 to 6 aircraft; normal complement 2 later increased to 3
Complement:	107

Name	Builder	Laid down	Launched	Completed	Fate
ANSWALD	Bremer Vulkan, Vegesack	?	September, 1909	?	BU 1933

Answald with a Friedrichshafen floatplane taxiing alongside and another atop the aft hangar. Unlike hangars on British carriers, which opened to the stern, those of the German vessels opened to the side. *Peter M Grosz collection*

This cargo-passenger vessel was leased from the Hamburg-Bremer Afrika Linie on 3 August 1914 for conversion to the German navy's first seaplane carrier by the Danzig Kaiserliche Werft. She was additionally fitted as a general depot ship for torpedo craft, carrying

coal, oil, fire brick and feed water, and equipped with an extensive sick bay.

Sea trials carried out from Wilhelmshaven during 25–28 August proved her unsuitable for North Sea work because of low speed and instability caused by high freeboard of the hangars. She was returned for modifications including increased ballasting, mounting of armament and increase of aircraft capacity from two to three. She was commissioned as a fleet auxiliary on 17 July 1915, designated *Flugzeugmutterschiffe* I (FS I).

From 20 August 1915 to 12 May 1916 *Answald*

based mainly at Libau in the Baltic, and after that until the end of the war mainly at Swindmuende, her aircraft being employed principally in routine coastal patrol.

Surrendered to Britain in 1919, she re-entered mercantile service under the red ensign, and was renamed *Vulcan City*. She was scrapped in 1933.

Aircraft operated by *Answald* and other German carriers of World War I were principally Friedrichshafen floatplanes, ranging from the FF29 model of 1914 to the FF64 of 1918, but most were various versions of the FF33 series

Santa Elena, basically similar to *Answald* but with different placement of hangars. *WZ-Bilddienst, Wilhelmshaven*

SANTA ELENA (FS II)

Displacement:	7415grt (7534 tonnes)
Dimensions:	452ft × 55ft × 23ft
	(137.3m × 16.7m × 7m)
Machinery:	1 set quadruple expansion, 3 boilers, 1 shaft, 2800ihp = 11kts
Armament	2–3.4in/45 (88mm) AA
Aircraft	
arrangements:	forward hangar 57ft 6in (17.5m) × 39ft (12m), aft hangar 55ft (16.75m) × 39ft (12m); 2 to 6 aircraft; normal complement 3 later increased to 4
Complement:	122

Name	Builder	Laid down	Launched	Completed	Fate
SANTA ELENA	Blohm & Voss, Hamburg	?	16 November, 1907	?	BU 1945

A cargo-passenger vessel, *Santa Elena* was leased from the Hamburg-Sudamerikan Dampfschiffahrts Gesellschaft on 3 August 1914 for conversion along the same lines as *Answald*, also by the Danzig Kaiserliche Werft. Like that vessel, and for the same reasons, she proved unsatisfactory during sea trials and was further modified in early 1915, aircraft capacity being enlarged from three to four, and armament mounted.

She was commissioned as *Flugzeugmutterschiffe II* (FS II) on 2 July 1915 and was based at Libau from 3 August 1915. Her aircraft were active along the Courland coast and the Gulf of Riga during 1915–17, flying reconnaissance and bombing missions against Russian shore installations and ships in support of German land and sea operations. From 12 October to 20 October 1918, *Santa Elena* took part in Operation

Albion, the seizure of the islands in the Gulf of Riga.

In late November 1918, she was transferred to Ore Sound for surveillance of neutral shipping. From 12 February to 7 November 1918, she was based at Wilhelmshaven to provide aerial support for North Sea minelaying and minesweeping operations.

Santa Elena was surrendered to the United States on 19 September 1919 and transferred that year to British mercantile service without change of name. She came under French ownership in 1920, and in 1922 was renamed *Linois*. She became the Italian *Orvieto* in 1924 and in September 1943 was taken over by the German Mediterranean Sea Transportation Service. Sunk at Marseilles in August 1944, either by air attack or scuttling, she was raised and scrapped in 1945.

GLYNDWR

Displacement:	2245grt (2464 tonnes)
Dimensions:	331ft × 44ft × 19ft
	(100.7m × 13.4m × 58m)
Machinery:	1 set triple expansion, 2 boilers, 1 shaft, 1600ihp = 10kts
Armament:	2–4pdr replaced in 1915 by 2–4.1in/45 (105mm)
Aircraft arrangements:	no hangars installed; aircraft handled on deck; 2 to 4 aircraft
Complement:	91

Name	Builder	Laid down	Launched	Completed	Fate
GLYNDWR, ex-CRAIGRONALD	A Rodger & Company, Port Glasgow	?	October 1904	?	BU 1955

The Scarisbrick Steamship Company's *Glyndwr* (the name was changed from *Craigronald* in 1911) was interned at Danzig at the start of World War I and modified to carry seaplanes by the Kaiserliche Werft there. She commissioned on 16 December 1914, strangely without a change of name, as a seaplane pilot training vessel with two aircraft. She was further modified, with aircraft capacity increased to four, and a heavier armament mounted, in January 1915,

recommissioning on the 11th of that month.

Glyndwr operated in the Baltic in early 1915, based at Memel from 28 March to 22 May and thereafter at Libau, her aircraft performing the same missions as *Santa Elena*'s. She was severely damaged by striking

Glyndwr with a pair of Friedrichshafen seaplanes aboard the bare decks from which she handled aircraft. *Courtesy of Edgar Meos*

14.　*Oswald*, best-equipped of the German converted seaplane carriers. *Author's collection*

a mine on 4 June and was laid up under repair at Danzig for six months, recommissioning 16 December 1915.

The repair was unsatisfactory, and she returned for further work that kept her inactive until 9 April 1916, when she was stationed in Ore Sound. Still defective from the mine damage, she ceased aviation service in September 1916 and served as a searchlight barrier vessel and mine depot ship until 1918.

She was surrendered to Great Britain on 21 January 1919, given complete repair and re-entered mercantile service under the name *Akenside*. Sold to a Greek firm in the 1920s and renamed *Agia Varvara*, she survived World War II and was broken up sometime in the mid-1950s.

OSWALD (FS III)

Displacement:	3657grt (3715 tonnes)
Dimensions:	370ft × 50ft × 22ft
	(112.5m × 15.3m × 6.7m)
Machinery:	1 set triple expansion, 2 boilers, 1 shaft, 2200ihp = 10kts
Armament:	2–3.4in/45 (88mm) AA
Aircraft	
arrangements:	forward hangar 64ft (20.8m) × 44ft (14.5m), aft hangar 68ft (22.5m) × 45ft (15m); 4 aircraft
Complement:	95

Name	Builder	Laid down	Launched	Completed	Fate
OSWALD, ex-OSWESTRY	J L Thompson & Sons, Sunderland	?	November 1905	?	Sunk by US aircraft, 25.7.1945

The Imperial Steamship Company's cargo vessel *Oswestry* was, like *Glyndwr*, interned at Danzig at the start of the war but was ignored until the summer of 1917, when she was taken over for use as a minesweeper depot ship, renamed *Oswald*. From 19 September 1917 she was employed as a transport, taking part in Operation Albion until 8 November.

She was converted to a seaplane carrier at the Danzig Kaiserliche Werft during February–July 1918, commissioning on 17 July as *Flugzeugmutterschiffe III* (FS III). From 21 July until October she was stationed in Ore Sound and the southern Kattegat, attached to Destroyer Flotilla IV and employed mainly to provide aerial escort to submarines returning from patrol.

Surrendered to Britain on 18 December 1919, she was sold to the Japanese Dairen Kisen KK in 1924 and renamed *Eian Maru*. She was sunk by American aircraft on 25 July 1945.

Incorporating experience gained from previous carrier conversions and operations, *Oswald* was probably the best-equipped German aviation vessel of World War I, but like the other conversions was too handicapped by low speed for fleet work, and also entered service too late to see much operational use.

ADELINE HUGO STINNES 3

Displacement:	2709grt (2752.5 tonnes)
Dimensions:	343ft × 45ft × 19ft 6in
	(104.2m × 13.8m × 6m)
Machinery:	1 set triple expansion, 2 boilers, 1 shaft, 1700ihp = 11kts
Armament:	nil
Aircraft	
arrangements:	nil; 3 aircraft
Complement:	27

Name	Builder	Laid down	Launched	Completed	Fate
ADELINE HUGO STINNES 3	Bremer Vulkan, Vegesack	?	?	1909	BU 1964

Built for Adeline Hugo Stinnes 3 Dampfschiffahrts Gesellschaft, this vessel was taken over by the German navy in 1914 as a collier for torpedo craft. At some unspecified time, three aircraft were added to her equipment (where and for what purpose is unknown) with no modification for their carriage or operation

She was surrendered to Belgium on 31 July 1919, renamed *Tervaete* in 1921, altered in 1926, after a change of ownership, to *Willem Rene*. In 1933 she was chartered by the Soviet government to transport timber to Cardiff, later being sold to a Finnish owner and renamed *Myllykoski*. She was scrapped in 1964, the last survivor of the World War I aviation vessels, and the most obscure.

A postwar view of *Adeline Hugo Stinnes 3*, probably the least-known aviation vessel of World War I. *Drüppel*

STUTTGART

Displacement:	3413t (3469 tonnes) normal, 3938t (4002 tonnes) full load
Dimensions:	386ft × 44ft × 17ft 7in
	(117.4m × 13.3m × 5.4m)
Machinery:	2 sets vertical triple expansion, 11 boilers, 2 shafts, 13,898ihp = 24kts 4170 nm at 12kts
Armament:	originally 10–4.1in/40 (105mm) 10 × 1, altered in 1918 to 4–4.1in/40 (105mm) 4 × 1 and 2–3.4in/45 (88mm) AA 2 × 1; 2–17.7in (450mm) TT
Armour:	deck 2in (51mm), conning tower 4in (102mm)
Aircraft arrangements:	hangar 65ft (20m) × 39ft (12m), 2 derricks, 2 cranes; 3 aircraft
Complement:	350

Name	Builder	Laid down	Launched	Completed	Fate
STUTTGART	Kaiserliche Werft, Danzig	1905	22.9.1906	1908	BU, 1920(?)

Stuttgart after her conversion to a seaplane carrier in early 1918. The white circles painted on forecastle and quarterdeck are aircraft identification symbols. *Peter M Grosz collection*

The conversion of this light cruiser represents the German navy's sole creation in two world wars of a seagoing aviation vessel capable of fleet work.

One of the three-ship *Stettin* class, *Stuttgart* was employed as a gunnery training vessel before being attached to the High Seas Fleet at the outbreak of war. She took part in the battle of Jutland as a unit of Scouting Group IV, then was laid up at Wilhelmshaven for a long refit.

Her transformation into a seaplane carrier was the result of a request in early December 1917 from the High Seas Fleet command to the Imperial Naval Office that one or more cruisers be converted to provide more extensive aerial reconnaissance for the minesweeping and minelaying operations that were extending deeper into the Heligoland Bight. A report assessing the work of the converted merchantmen, until that time during the war (including use during Operation Albion), recommended construction of a special aviation vessel. Both documents noted the greatest handicap of the converted ships: their slow speed.

Construction was ruled out because of the time it would require, but the Naval Office began a study of the possible conversion of one or more of the light cruisers *Strassburg*, *Kolberg*, *Augsburg*, *Stuttgart*, *Stettin* and *Danzig*. Consideration also was given to six possibly suitable merchant vessels, ranging from the giant 52,117grt *Imperator* to the 1916grt coastal steamer *Kaiser*, all capable of about 18kts. The merchantmen were eliminated as either too large or too small, with inadequate speed, and conversion of the cruisers was frowned upon because of the reduction of firepower it would necessitate.

However, when the High Seas Fleet request was renewed on 29 December 1917 as a matter of urgency, officialdom relented and on 20 January 1918 the conversion of *Stuttgart* and *Stettin* was authorized.

Whether work on *Stettin* was delayed until operational lessons from *Stuttgart* could be learned, or whether it began at all, is unclear, but in any event she was not converted.

Work on *Stuttgart* started in late January at the Wilhelmshaven Kaiserliche Werft. A steel girder canvas-as-shielded hangar was placed aft of her third funnel, seaplane-handling derricks and cranes were installed, six of her 4.1in guns were landed and replaced by two 3.4in AA guns on the forecastle. She was commissioned on 16 May 1918 as flagship, Officer Commanding North Sea Aerial Forces, and took part in minesweeping operations as a unit of the reconnaissance forces headed by Admiral Franz von Hipper.

Inactive after the fleet uprisings of late 1918, *Stuttgart* was stricken on 5 November 1919, surrendered to Britain on 20 July 1920 and subsequently scrapped at Teignmouth, probably that year.

Other projects

Although *Stuttgart* could carry three seaplanes, the hangar accommodated only two. The third, carried on deck, could not be employed during bad weather, and two planes were considered an inadequate number for effective reconnaissance to detect approach of enemy ships during sweeping operations. Consequently, the High Seas Fleet command suggested on 12 August that, instead of *Stettin*, a larger cruiser, able to carry more aircraft, be converted; specifically mentioned was the old armoured cruiser *Roon*, then in use as a cadet training ship in the Baltic.

A consultation between naval aviators and construction experts at the Kiel Kaiserliche Werft arrived at a conversion plan for *Roon* that would have permitted her to carry eight to ten seaplanes, handled

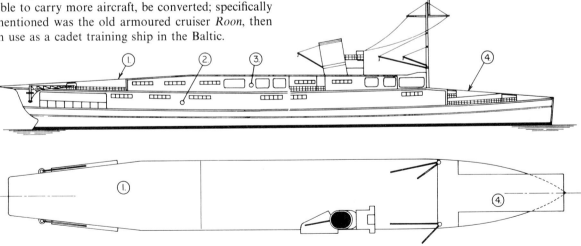

A representation of the proposed redesign of *Ausonia* as a flight-deck carrier, based upon and developed from plans published in *Schiffbau* No 2 1920. *Drawings by Stephen McLaughlin*

1. LANDING DECK
2. SEAPLANE HANGAR DECK
3. AEROPLANE HANGAR DECK
4. TAKEOFF PLATFORM

Friedrichshafen FF.29 floatplane No 201 aboard
U12 at Zeebrugge, 6 January 1915. *Courtesy of
Walter Forstmann*

by four derricks, in a large aft hangar, with armament
reduced and rearranged to consist of six 5.9in (150mm)
LA guns 6 x 1 and six 3.4in (88mm) AA guns 6 x 1.

Some initial approval must have been given to this
suggestion, for on 16 September the Baltic naval
command was told of it, and advised to seek housing
elsewhere for the cadets on *Roon*. Some material for
the conversion was apparently stockpiled, although,
reportedly, with difficulty because of the priority being
given to submarine construction. Whatever the case,
the project was cancelled the following month without
any work having been started on the cruiser.

At the same time as *Roon's* conversion was proposed, the idea was advanced that the North Sea
aerial reconnaissance problem might be solved by
equipping a number of *Sperrbrechern* (auxiliary minesweepers) with seaplanes and mooring them in the
bight as stationary aircraft depot ships. At least one
of these vessels, *Steigerwald*, did carry a seaplane at
an undetermined date in 1918, which may have been
an experiment along these lines.

On 11 October 1918 the naval air command came
up with the first proposal for a German flight-deck
carrier, advocating that the merchantmen *Bremen*
and *Königin Luise*, both around 13,000grt, 500ft and

15kts, be converted in this fashion to carry ten aircraft
each. If a larger ship were desired, the incomplete liner
Ausonia was suggested. She was under construction
for an Italian firm at Hamburg by Blohm & Voss at
the start of the war, and still on a slip.

Whether it was known by the advocates of this
proposal or whether by coincidence, *Ausonia* had
already been considered as a flight-deck carrier by a
naval aviator, Leutnant zur See Jürgen Reimpell,
in a doctoral dissertation written for the Berlin
Technische Hochschule. It was a good scheme,
featuring a funnel and small pilothouse offset to
starboard of a landing deck that extended over about
four-fifths of the ship's length with an overhang at the
stern. Below the landing deck was a hangar dec' for
aircraft, opening to a forward platform permitting
takeoff directly from the hangar, as would be the case
initially in the postwar British *Furious*, *Glorious* and
Courageous and the Japanese *Kaga* and *Akagi*. It is
unclear whether a lift was proposed; more likely the
aircraft were to be transferred from the landing deck
by booms on two parallel masts forward of it.

Below the aircraft deck was a seaplane hangar deck,
these craft to be handled by two large derricks at the
stern. It was calculated that thirteen fixed-wing or
nineteen folding-wing aircraft could be carried. No
provision seems to have been made for armament.

At this point in the war, all these schemes were
academic, but the Imperial Naval Office gave them

Commerce raider *Wolf* at Kiel, February 1918, after returning from her long and adventurous cruise. Her aircraft is displayed on deck aft of the mainmast. *Peter M Grosz collection*

Wolf's Friedrichshafen FF.33e on deck after the raider's return to Germany. The insignia, serial number and nickname have been painted on for display; the aircraft carried no markings during its operational career. It is typical of the Friedrichshafen series, which were the principal aircraft of the German carriers. *Peter M Grosz collection*

all due consideration and rejected them in toto, including conversion of *Roon* on the grounds that she was too valuable as a training ship.

Reimpell won a degree with his dissertation after the armistice, but plans for a German flight-deck carrier went into limbo and when the idea was revived, years later, Japanese design assistance was sought.

Two more German aeronaval combinations from World War I are worth noting. One was the first attempt to mate aircraft and submarines, when on 6 January 1915 *U12* stood out from Zeebrugge harbour with a Friedrichshafen FF.29 twin-float seaplane carried athwartship on the forward deck. This was a

scheme concocted by *U12*'s captain, Kapitänleutnant Walter Forstmann, and Oberleutnant zur See Friedrich von Arnauld de la Perrière, commander of the Zeebrugge naval air contingent, who was at the controls of the seaplane that morning.

The plan was to extend the range of von Arnauld's seaplanes to reach targets in England by carrying them to striking distance on submarines that would trim down until the aircraft floated free for takeoff, and this was the first operational test of the idea after experiments in harbour proved its feasibility.

It worked almost as planned, although a rising swell forced an earlier takeoff than scheduled, to prevent the plane being torn from its crude deck fastenings. Von Arnauld and his observer flew to the Kentish coast, apparently unseen by anyone ashore. A return rendezvous between aircraft and submarine was planned, but because of worsening weather both made for Zeebrugge independently.

The reaction of higher authorities to whom a report of the experiment was forwarded was unfavorable to say the least, and a sternly worded directive was passed down forbidding a repetition.

Much later in the war it was proposed to equip some of the large cruiser submarines under construction with aircraft, and at least two small seaplanes were designed for this purpose. However, nothing came of the idea and it is doubtful whether anything would have, even if the armistice had not intervened. Still, it is interesting to note that, in June 1918, air raid precautions were taken in the Greater New York City area and along the New Jersey coast for fear that the German submarines then operating off the US coast were carrying bomb-laden seaplanes.

Far more successful was the work of a seaplane carried by the disguised commerce raider *Wolf* during her famous 1917 cruise. A twin-float Friedrichshafen FF.33e nicknamed *Wolfchen* (Little Wolf or Wolf Cub), greatly assisted the raider by spotting mercantile prey for her; and, by bombing or threatening to bomb it, helped in several captures. On at least four occasions, the seaplane can probably be credited with capturing ships entirely on its own.

During *Wolf*'s sojourn in the Indian Ocean and South Pacific the seaplane made between 54 and 56 flights, surely the greatest number by any shipboard aircraft during World War I. Keeping it in flying shape during the long cruise under some of the worst possible conditions of climate and weather constituted an epic of aircraft maintenance.

The lessons learned from this combination of ship and aircraft were applied by the seaplane-carrying German surface commerce raiders of World War II.

Great Britain

The Royal Navy can be credited with introducing aerial devices into European maritime warfare in 1806, when the dashing Lord Thomas Cochrane flew kites from his 32-gun frigate *Pallas* to spread propaganda leaflets over the French coast. Three years earlier, Rear Admiral Charles Henry Knowles had submitted a scheme to the Admiralty for lofting a balloon from a ship to reconnoitre French invasion preparations at Brest. This was ignored, and was the last serious proposal for a British aviation vessel for more than a century.

The Royal Navy entered the aviation age in 1909 with the decision to construct a rigid airship. It was appropriately nicknamed *Mayfly*, and it broke up before ever going aloft. What was to prove a far more decisive step was taken in 1911, when four officers were detailed to take advantage of a private offer of aircraft flight training. One of them, Lieutenant (later RAF Colonel) Charles R Samson, made the first takeoff from a British ship on 10 January 1912, flying a Short pusher biplane off a sloping track erected over the forward turret and forecastle of the battleship *Africa*, moored off Sheerness.

A few months later, the battleship *Hibernia* was fitted with a similar but less angled track, on which it transported the same Short and the Short S41 floatplane – the Royal Navy's first seaplane – to a naval review at Weymouth. On 2 May 1912

Short S.27 T.2 aboard *Hibernia*, probably off Weymouth. While the *Africa*'s launching track was angled downward toward the bow, that of *Hibernia* was nearly flat. *Courtesy of Short Brothers and Harland*

Facing page: Short S.27 serial number T.2 aboard *Africa* with Charles R Samson at the controls on 10 January 1912, shortly before the first aircraft takeoff from a British vessel. *Imperial War Museum*

(the date has often been given as 9 May but *Hibernia*'s log and Samson's flight log definitely establish it as 2 May) Samson flew the Short pusher off the trackway while *Hibernia* was steaming at $10\frac{1}{2}$kts – the first flight from a moving ship.

Between these two dates, a formal British air arm came into existence: the Royal Flying Corps, divided into a Military Wing, a Naval Wing, and a Central Flying School to train aviators for both. The Naval Wing quickly broke away, and began calling itself the Royal Naval Air Service (a title later made official). It trained pilots independently and acquired its own aircraft. In November, the Admiralty established an air department, and although the RNAS remained on paper a branch of the RFC

Samson lifting the Short off *Hibernia* in Weymouth Bay, 2 May 1912, in the first takeoff of an aeroplane from a moving vessel. The discernible bow wave proves movement, despite some denials that the ship was under way. *Courtesy of Short Brothers and Harland*

A closer view of the Short aboard *Hibernia* shows the slight slope of the launching track over the forward turret and the long boom fitted to the forecmast for handling the aircraft. *Author's collection*

The Short being hoisted aboard *Hibernia*, probably off Weymouth after the 2 May flight. This view shows how the landing gear wheels were obscured by the torpedo-shaped flotation bags – a shape that led some observers at the time to describe the aircraft as a seaplane. *Author's collection*

until 1915, it was *de facto* a naval appendage. An influential force behind its development and technical innovations was Winston Churchill, who became First Lord of the Admiralty in October 1911.

The first formal proposal for a British aviation vessel came in December 1912 from the shipbuilding firm of William Beardmore & Company, which submitted to the Admiralty a plan for what it called a 'parent ship for naval aeroplanes and torpedo-boat destroyers', which was, in essence, a flight-deck carrier, displacing 15,000t (15,241 tonnes) and measuring 450ft (148m) on the waterline × 110ft (36.1m). Amidships of a flush deck were two parallel superstructures, each with a funnel and mast, 220ft (72.3m) long, connected by a bridge spanning a 50ft (16.4m) deck between them. Each of these was to house three aircraft, with their wings stretching fore and aft, in separate compartments. They were to take off from the forward part of the deck, and land on the aft section. The deck between the superstructures was to be closed off in bad weather by what was called a hinged 'gate'. Four disassembled seaplanes were to be carried below, handled by cranes fore and aft of each superstructure. Armament was to be six 4in guns, and the ship was to have a large fuel oil capacity, a powerful wireless installation and spacious accommodation for ammunition and relief crews. Six more aeroplanes were to be stowed as spares.

With hindsight, it is clear that landing an aircraft on such a ship in the face of the buffeting of air, broken by the superstructure, and smoke pouring from the funnels would have been virtually impossible. The Board of Admiralty rejected the

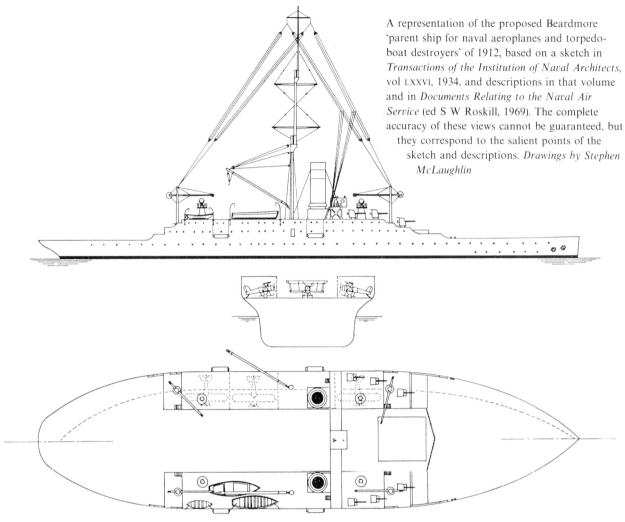

A representation of the proposed Beardmore 'parent ship for naval aeroplanes and torpedo-boat destroyers' of 1912, based on a sketch in *Transactions of the Institution of Naval Architects*, vol LXXVI, 1934, and descriptions in that volume and in *Documents Relating to the Naval Air Service* (ed S W Roskill, 1969). The complete accuracy of these views cannot be guaranteed, but they correspond to the salient points of the sketch and descriptions. *Drawings by Stephen McLaughlin*

Beardmore proposal not for this reason, for it was hardly suspected, but with the polite explanation that 'as sufficient experience had not yet been gained with hydroplanes working from a ship at sea to enable naval requirements to be definitely stated, it was considered inadvisable to proceed further with the matter at present'. The cumbersome terms 'hydroplane' and 'hydroaeroplane' were soon replaced by 'seaplane', a word coined by Winston Churchill.

A valuable start to gaining that experience was made the next year with the commissioning, on 7 May 1913, of the cruiser *Hermes* as a parent ship for seaplanes during the annual naval manoeuvres. A two-track platform was installed over the forecastle for takeoff by seaplanes on trollies, a canvas shelter rigged on the quarterdeck for seaplanes, and a long aircraft-handling boom fitted on the lower mainmast.

For the manoeuvres scheduled in July, two aircraft were embarked – a French Borel float monoplane and the wireless-equipped Short S.64, a twin-float, two-place biplane that was the general prototype for a long series of aircraft that the pioneer British aeronautical firm of Short Bros was to provide for the Royal Navy. It had folding wings, a patented feature that reduced their 56ft span to 12ft for handier shipboard accommodation, and which resulted in the type being nicknamed Folder. This innovation was a major advance toward making aircraft amenable to shipboard carriage, and is a feature of most carrier aircraft, to this day.

Hermes outfitted as a seaplane carrier at Sheerness in 1913 for the naval manoeuvres of that year. A tracked takeoff platform extends over the forecastle, an aircraft handling boom is installed on the foremast and there are canvas aircraft shelters fore and aft. *P A Vicary*

Caudron amphibian serial number 55 taking off from *Hermes* on 28 July 1913. *Courtesy of Dr A Hewlett via Michael H Goodall*

The Borel was damaged in a gale before the manoeuvres began, and was replaced with a French Caudron G.III amphibian whose wheels were recessed into its twin floats – the same type of aircraft used the next year in takeoff experiments on the French *Foudre* (qv).

Between 5 July and 6 October, *Hermes*' aircraft made approximately thirty flights, before, during and after the manoeuvres. The Caudron was flown off the platform twice while the cruiser was under way, on 28 July, landing at Great Yarmouth, and

A Sopwith Baby, piloted by Flight Sublieutenant Robert W Peel, in flight over shipping in Mudros harbour, Lemnos, in late 1917 or early 1918. The Sopwith Schneider and its near companion, the re-engined Baby, were, together with the Short 184, the most widely employed British floatplanes of World War I. The Baby seen here was the one in which Peel unsuccessfully attacked the battle cruiser *Goeben* in early 1918. *Courtesy of Robert W Peel*

Empress as she originally appeared as a prewar cross-Channel packet. *Courtesy of D K Brown*

on 3 September, landing at Cromarty. Its wheels made the use of trollies unnecessary. It has often been asserted that these takeoffs played a part in the genesis of the aircraft carrier, but in fact they only duplicated the battleship experiments of the year before. Far more significant was the demonstration that sustained operation of aircraft from shipboard was feasible under service conditions, that wireless communication was essential for aerial reconnaissance at sea, and that the folding wing was an immensely useful feature for shipboard aircraft.

Although *Hermes*' aircraft failed to achieve anything that had any bearing on the conduct of the 1913 manoeuvres, this longest sustained test of shipboard aviation before World War I was highly influential in shaping Royal Navy attitudes toward aircraft at sea. It was the beginning of the developments that would end in November 1918 with the British Navy possessing the world's greatest naval air strength and more aviation vessels and aircraft-equipped ships than all the other navies of the world combined.

Hermes did not live to see that day; paid off into reserve in December 1913, she was recommissioned on 31 August 1914 as an RNAS transport and supply ship, having retained most of her aviation appurtenances. She was sunk by *U27* on 31 October 1914 off Dunkirk, but she had paved the way.

Special note on armament of British carriers. The armanent of many of these vessels varied during the war, mainly because of the addition of anti-aircraft guns. The armament listed in the tables is that which was mounted in 1918. In most cases, it has been impossible to determine the calibre (ie, bore-to-barrel ratio).

Empress as originally converted to a seaplane carrier, with canvas hangars fore and aft. *Engadine* and *Riviera* were fitted identically during their first conversions. *Imperial War Museum*

RIVIERA

Displacement:	2550t (2560.9 tonnes), 1675grt
Dimensions:	313ft pp, 316ft oa × 41ft × 13ft 8in (mean)
	(102.9m × 103.9m × 13.4m × 4.5m)
Machinery:	3 sets direct-drive turbines, 6 boilers, 3 shafts, 11,000shp = 20.5kts; 860nm at 10kts. Coal: 400t (464 tonnes)
Armament:	4–12pdr/8 or 12cwt, 2–3pdr/4 or 5cwt AA
Aircraft arrangements:	canvas hangars fore and aft replaced in 1915 by permanent hangar aft; derrick forward, 2 jib cranes aft; 4 aircraft
Complement:	(1918): 197 including 53 aviation personnel

Official Admiralty sources give displacement of *Riviera* and *Engadine* as identical but there was in fact a slight disparity.

ENGADINE

Displacement:	2550t (2560.9 tonnes), 1676grt
Dimensions:	as *Riviera*
Machinery:	as *Riviera* except 13,800shp = 21.5kts
Armament:	as *Riviera*
Aircraft arrangements:	as *Riviera*
Complement	(1918): as *Riviera*

Name	Builder	Laid down	Launched	Completed	Fate
RIVIERA	William Denny & Brothers, Dumbarton	?	1.4.1911	1911	BU, 1957
ENGADINE	as above	?	23.9.1911	1911 or 1912	Mined, Manila Bay, December 1941

Official Admiralty, and other sources give *Empress* as identical to *Riviera* and *Engadine*, but she differed in the particulars given below, and probably somewhat also in aircraft arrangements and complement.

EMPRESS

Displacement:	1694grt (1721 tonnes)
Dimensions:	323ft oa × 41ft × 15ft (mean)
	(106.2m × 13.4m × 4.9m)
Machinery:	3 sets direct-drive turbines, 6 boilers, 3 shafts, 11,000shp = 18kts. Coal: 425t (493 tonnes)

All other particulars as *Riviera* and *Engadine*

Name	Builder	Laid down	Launched	Completed	Fate
EMPRESS	William Denny & Brothers, Dumbarton	?	13.4.1907	1907	BU, 1933

These three cross-Channel packets of the South Eastern & Chatham Railway Company were requisitioned by the Admiralty – hired and later purchased – on 11 August 1914. *Riviera* and *Engadine* were converted for carrying seaplanes at the Chatham Dockyard with installation of canvas shelters accommodating one aircraft foreward and two aft, handling booms and armaments of two or three 2-pdr guns. The work was completed, and sea trials run, by 1 September for *Engadine* and 6 September for *Riviera*.

They were originally scheduled to join the main body of the Grand Fleet for aerial reconnaissance work, but instead were assigned to the Harwich Force and took part in unsuccessful attempts to bomb a German airship base from October to February 1915. The so-called Cuxhaven Raid took place on 25 December 1914.

As a result of experience gained in these operations, both ships were taken in hand by the Cunard Steamship Company at Liverpool for more extensive modification in which permanent aft hangars replaced the canvas shelters and anti-aircraft armament was added. Work on *Riviera* lasted from 14 February to 7 April 1915 and on *Engadine* from 10 February to 23 March.

After this remodelling *Riviera* was assigned to the Dover Patrol and was active in operations off the

Engadine after her second conversion, with the large aft hangar that also characterized Riviera and Empress. J M Bruce/G S Leslie collection

Riviera hoisting a Sopwith Baby at Dartmouth, date unknown. What appears to be a Short 184 is on deck with wings extended. This view shows well the spaciousness of the hangar. Courtesy of Fisher Nautical

Belgian coast, based at Dover and Dunkirk, from mid-1915 to July 1917, when she was stationed at Falmouth for anti-submarine duty. In early 1918, she was assigned to the Mediterranean where she spent the rest of the war, based mainly at Malta.

She was returned to her owner in 1919, sold to Southern Railway in 1923 and then to Burns and Laird Lines in 1932, renamed Lairds Isle. Requisitioned again by the Admiralty in September 1939, she served as a torpedo training ship, armed boarding vessel and infantry landing ship. She was returned to her owner in 1945 and sold for scrapping in 1957.

Engadine, upon completion of her remodelling at

Liverpool, was stationed at Granton from July to October 1915 and was then attached to the Battle Cruiser Fleet at Rosyth, where in late October she carried out tests proving the feasibility of high-speed towing of kite balloons. She continued as BCF aviation vessel until late 1917, taking part in North Sea operations. *Engadine* was stationed in the light cruiser scouting line at the opening of the Battle of Jutland on 31 May 1916 and launched a Short 184 floatplane for a reconnaissance flight that although fairly successful had no influence on events. Later she took in tow the badly damaged armoured cruiser *Warrior* and rescued her crew when the cruiser was abandoned.

In early 1918 she was transferred to the Mediterranean with the other older carriers and spent the rest of the war there, based at Malta.

Engadine was returned to her owners in December 1919, sold to the Southern Railway in 1923, chartered by Instone Line in 1932 and sold to Fernandez Hermanos Inc in the Philippines in 1933. Renamed *Corregidor*, she was sunk by a mine in Manila Bay in December 1941 with considerable loss of life.

Aircraft operated by *Riviera* and *Engadine* included Short Folder, Short Admiralty Types 74, 135, 830 and 184 and Sopwith Schneider and Baby.

Empress was employed as a Royal Naval Air Service transport and dispatch vessel in August 1914, taking *matériel* for the RNAS Eastchurch Squadron to Ostend that month. From 30 August to 30 September she was converted to a carrier along the lines of *Riviera* and *Engadine* at the Chatham Dockyard and joined them at Harwich in October. She was their associate in the 1914 operations, including the Cuxhaven Raid.

She was modified with the same type of aft hangar as the other two ships by Cunard at Liverpool, from 9 May to 18 July 1915, and then stationed at Queenstown for a time. Assigned to the East Indies and Egypt Seaplane Squadron at Port Said, she arrived there in January 1916. In April she was detached for operations off the Bulgarian coast, based at Aegean ports. She rejoined the EI & E Squadron after refitting at Genoa and was active in its operations off the Sinai-Syrian coast until November. From January 1918 to the end of the war she was used mainly for anti-submarine work, based first at Port Said and then at Gibraltar.

Empress was returned to her owners in November 1919, sold in 1923 to the Southern Railway and resold later that year to the French Société Anonyme de Gérance et d'Armement. She was scrapped in France in 1933.

Aircraft operated by *Empress* included Short Admiralty Types 74 and 184, Sopwith Schneider and Baby and Fairey Hamble Baby.

ANNE

Displacement:	4083t (4148.6 tonnes)				
Dimensions:	367ft 1in × 47ft 7in × 27ft 3in				
	(111.8m × 14.5m × 8.3m)				
Machinery:	triple expansion, 1 shaft, ?ihp = 11kts				
Armament:	1 MG augmented by 1–12pdr/8 or 12 cwt LA later replaced by 1–12pdr/8 or 12cwt AA				
Aircraft arrangements:	canvas windscreens; 1–3 aircraft				
Complement:	?				

Name	Builder	Laid down	Launched	Completed	Fate
ANNE, ex-AENNE RICKMERS	Rickmers AG, Bremerhaven	?	?	1911	BU 1958

This cargo vessel built for Rickmers Reismuhlen, Reederei & Schiffbau AG was seized at Port Said in August 1914. She was pressed into service as a makeshift seaplane carrier in January 1915 for reconnaissance beyond the range of land-based aircraft, operating under the red ensign with a mixed naval-civilian crew and retaining her original name. Her aircraft were the Nieuport floatplanes disembarked at Port Said by the French carrier *Foudre* (qv) with French pilots and British observers. Their observation was largely responsible for the deployment of military and naval units that defeated the Turkish thrust toward the Suez Canal in early 1915.

She operated off the Sinai, Syrian and Turkish coasts until 11 March 1915, when she was torpedoed by the Turkish torpedo boat *Demir Hisar*. She was deliberately grounded at Mudros for temporary shoring up and refloated on 12 May. She proceeded to Alexandria for permanent repair, completed on 18 June.

After further operations off the Turkish coast in July, she was commissioned as an RN vessel on 5 August 1915, renamed *Anne*, receiving a Royal Navy crew and armed with a 12pdr LA gun. She subsequently served mainly with French forces until attached to the East Indies and Egypt Seaplane Squadron in January 1916.

Anne handed over her Nieuports to the French carrier *Campinas* (qv) at Malta on 9 May, and, the same month, had her 12pdr replaced with an AA gun of the same calibre. Now equipped with British aircraft, she operated with the EI & E squadron in

Anne, still bearing the name *Aenne Rickmers*, aground at Mudros for temporary repair of torpedo damage in early 1915. Her aircraft have been removed. *Author's collection*

the eastern Mediterranean, Aegean and Red Sea until paid off on 8 August 1917. From 29 January 1918 until the end of the war she served as a collier under the red ensign, managed by F C Strick & Company.

She was sold to a Greek firm in 1922 and renamed *Ithaki*, sold to a Romanian firm in 1939 and renamed *Moldova*, transferred to Panamanian registry in 1942 and sold to Wallen & Company, Panama, in 1949. Her ownership is difficult to trace after that, but she was renamed *Jagrahat* in 1954, reverting to *Moldova* in 1955, and was scrapped at Hong Kong in 1958.

In addition to the Nieuports, aircraft operated by *Anne* during 1915–17 included Short Admiralty Type 184 and Sopwith Schneider and Baby.

RAVEN II

Displacement:	4706grt (4781.6 tonnes)
Dimensions:	394ft 5in × 51ft 6in × 27ft 6in
	(119m × 16m × 8.3m)
Machinery:	quadruple expansion, probably 1 shaft, ?ihp = 10kts
Armament:	1–12pdr/8 or 12cwt LA
Aircraft arrangements:	canvas windscreens, 1–6 aircraft
Complement:	?

Name	Builder	Laid down	Launched	Completed	Fate
RAVEN II, ex-RABENFELS	Swan, Hunter & Wigham Richardson, Newcastle	?	?	December, 1903	?

As *Rabenfels* of the Deutsche Dampfschiffahrts-Gesellschaft 'Hansa', this cargo vessel was seized at Port Said along with *Aenne Rickmers* while en route from Rotterdam to Bombay.

Taken over in December to carry aircraft, she operated in the same manner as *Aenne Rickmers* with a naval-civilian crew under the red ensign and ex-*Foudre* Nieuports flown by French pilots with British observers. She took *Aenne Rickmers*' seaplanes off

that damaged vessel at Mudros in March. On 12 June 1915 she was commissioned as a Royal Navy ship and renamed *Raven II*.

For the rest of 1915, her career paralleled that of *Anne*, operating principally with French forces, and she was assigned with *Anne* to the East Indies and Egypt Seaplane Squadron in January 1916, operating in the eastern Mediterranean, Aegean and Red Sea. She was damaged by a bomb from a German aircraft

on 1 September 1916 at Port Said. With the French cruiser *Pothuau*, *Raven II* cruised in the Indian Ocean from 16 March to 10 June 1917 in an unsuccessful search for the German commerce raider *Wolf*.

She was paid off in late 1917 and engaged in mercantile service from January 1918 to the end of the war, renamed *Ravenrock* and managed by Grahams & Company. She was sold to British Dominions Steamship Company in 1923 and resold that year to Karafuto KKK, Japan, which renamed her *Heiyei Maru No. 7*. In 1935 she was sold to Inui KKK, which in 1938 altered the name to *Heiei Maru No. 7*. She

Raven II, date and location unknown, but probably *c*1917. The Japanese ensign is puzzling, but is probably being flown in honour of one or more of the Japanese vessels that assisted in convoy escort in the Mediterranean. *Author's collection*

Ben-my-Chree, probably at a late stage of her career. The takeoff platform has been removed. *Courtesy of P H Liddle*

was lost in the Pacific during World War II, but the date and circumstances are unknown.

Anne and *Raven II* received only the crudest of modifications to suit them for the carrier role. Their aircraft, protected only by canvas screens, were carried on decks or hatch covers and handled by ordinary cargo booms. But for arduousness and effectiveness of service their records are equalled by few if any other aviation vessels of World War I.

Raven II, in addition to carrying the same types of aircraft as *Anne*, also for a time operated the Short Admiralty Type 827.

BEN-MY-CHREE

Displacement:	3888t (3950.5 tonnes), 2651grt
Dimensions:	387ft oa × 47ft × 15ft (mean)
	(118m × 14.3m × 7.2m)
Machinery:	3 sets direct-drive turbines, 4 boilers, 3 shafts, 14,500shp = 24.5kts (exceeded in service).
	Coal: 552t (640.7 tonnes)
Armament:	4–12pdr/18cwt LA, 2–3pdr/4 or 5cwt AA; later augmented by 1–12pdr/18cwt AA, 1–3pdr/4 or 5cwt
	AA and 1–2pdr/? AA
Aircraft arrangements:	hangar aft, 1 derrick forward, 1 derrick aft, 4–6 aircraft
Complement:	172

Name	Builder	Laid down	Launched	Completed	Fate
BEN-MY-CHREE	Vickers Sons & Maxim, Barrow-in-Furness	?	23.4.1908	8.8.1908	Sunk by Turkish gunfire, 9.1.1917

This well-known and popular passenger vessel of the Isle of Man Steam Packet Company, bearing a traditional Manx name (Woman of My Heart), was hired by the Admiralty on 1 January 1915 for conversion to a seaplane carrier with a large aft hangar that was the prototype for succeeding British carriers. The work was done by Cammell, Laird & Company, Birkenhead, and she was commissioned as an RN vessel on 23 March 1915. She was originally outfitted with a dismountable forward launching platform for seaplanes on trollies.

Ben-my-Chree replaced *Empress* in the Harwich Force in April, and took part in operations off the German coast during May as the first British carrier to operate the Sopwith Schneider floatplane. The first attempt to fly one of these off the platform, on 11 May, was unsuccessful and the structure was removed later.

Ben-my-Chree replaced *Ark Royal* (qv) as fleet aviation vessel at the Dardanelles on 12 June 1915, carrying the first Short Type 184s to see shipboard use. She operated in that area for the rest of the year, and on 12 and 17 August her Shorts carried out the world's first aerial torpedo attacks. They were successful, but the results have been exaggerated and what they really accomplished, as well as the identities of the ships they sunk or damaged, remains uncertain.

A rare view of the forward platform on *Ben-my-Chree*, almost certainly in early 1915. The first attempt at using it was unsuccessful. *Fleet Air Arm Museum*

A typical Short Admiralty Type 184 floatplane (also unofficially known as the Short 225 from the rated horsepower of its original engine), the work horse of British naval aviation in World War I. Introduced in 1915 and going into combat for the first time aboard *Ben-my-Chree* at the Dardanelles, its later multi-engined versions served aboard every British aviation vessel, many other ships and probably every naval air station at least until 1919, from the Orkneys and Archangel to Aden and the Indian Ocean, and soldiered on in foreign service for even longer. Although designed for torpedo attack, of which it made the world's first, it was not successful in the role; the 184 seen here has the typical bomb rack between the floats. *Author's collection*

Ark Royal at Malta. The date may be postwar, but the carrier appears in her original configuration as completed in 1914. *J M Bruce/G S Leslie collection*

Ben-my-Chree became the flagship of the East Indies and Egypt Seaplane Squadron when it was formed at Port Said in January 1916 and was active in operations in the Aegean, the Red Sea and off the Syrian, Turkish, Bulgarian and North African coasts until the end of the year, save for a period in dry dock at Suez from 13 March to 25 April for repair of collision damage. On 9 January 1917, while lying in harbour at Castelorizo Island, she was set afire and sunk by Turkish artillery firing from the nearby mainland. The wreck was raised in 1921, towed to Piraeus and subsequently scrapped in Italy.

Before she gained the dubious distinction of becoming the only aviation vessel to be lost to enemy action in World War I, *Ben-my-Chree* had operated aircraft including the Sopwith Type 860, Schneider and Baby, and Short Types 830 and 184.

Ark Royal at Mudros late in the war; her appearance is unchanged except for a cluttered forecastle. *Author's collection*

ARK ROYAL/PEGASUS

Displacement:	7450t (7570 tonnes)
Dimensions:	366ft × 50ft × 18ft (mean) (111.5m × 15.5m × 5.4m)
Machinery:	1 set vertical triple expansion, 3 boilers, 1 shaft, 3000ihp = 11kts. Oil: 500t (580 tonnes)
Armament:	4–12pdr/8 or 12cwt, 2 MG
Aircraft arrangements:	belowdeck internal hangar 150ft (45m) × 54ft (13.7m), 2 3-ton steam cranes amidships; 7–12 aircraft
Complement:	(1918) 180 including 60 aviation personnel

Name	Builder	Laid down	Launched	Completed	Fate
ARK ROYAL, PEGASUS from 1935	Blyth Shipbuilding & Dry Docks Company, Blyth	7.11.1913	5.9.1914	10.12.1914	BU, 1950

Although *Ark Royal* was preceded operationally by five of the six British seaplane carriers previously described, she was in fact the Royal Navy's first aviation vessel *per se*. The Admiralty decision to acquire such a vessel stemmed from the *Hermes* experiments in 1913 and £81,000 was allotted for that purpose in the 1914–15 Navy Estimates.

The ship chosen, and purchased in May 1914, was a merchantman under construction at Blyth. Because of this mercantile origin, it has often been stated that Ark Royal was 'converted' for aviation service, but this is true in only the most tenuous sense of the word. She was originally designed as a conventional merchant ship, probably for use in the coal-for-grain trade between Britain and the Black Sea ports. As such, she had the usual mercantile internal and external layout with main superstructure, machinery and single funnel amidships, cargo holds fore and aft. She was radically redesigned by John H Narbeth, Assistant Director of Naval Construction, assisted by Charles J W Hopkins, with superstructure, machinery and funnel moved right aft, giving about two-thirds of the forward hull over to aircraft facilities. This configuration is responsible for another frequently published error; that *Ark Royal* was originally designed as a tanker.

The changes were so drastic that it can be stated *Ark Royal* was in fact designed and built as a carrier, the only remnants of her mercantile origins being keel and basic framing. Although she hardly looked like a flight-deck carrier, she incorporated for the first time in naval architecture features retained in such vessels to this day, notably an internal hangar enclosed by the hull in which aircraft were sheltered from the elements, as well as specially designed internal spaces for all the fuel, lubricants, ordnance, spares and machinery required for aircraft maintenance and operation.

A sliding hatch 40ft (13m) × 30ft (9.8m) gave access to the hangar, from which aircraft were hoisted by steam cranes. Below the waterline was a system of cellular water-ballast tanks designed to lower the ship's metacentric height to stabilise her while seaplanes were recovered from the sea, but it never may have been used in service.

From the cranes forward, the upper deck was unobstructed (anchor cables and machinery were installed on a lower deck) and without sheer. This feature may or may not have been intended to allow takeoff by seaplanes on trollies. Such takeoffs would

This aerial view of *Ark Royal*, taken by one of the aviators stationed at Mudros, shows her there in late 1917 or early 1918. A Sopwith Baby is on deck forward of the open hatch. *Courtesy of Robert W Peel*

Another aerial view of *Ark Royal*, again probably at Mudros, for the forecastle has become even more cluttered. The portside crane is working a Short 184 and another aircraft, its wings folded, can be seen through the open hatch. *Courtesy of P H Liddle*

seem to have been possible, and even feasible for aircraft with wheel undercarriage, as *Ark Royal*'s first commander was later to note. Despite some reports to the contrary, however, no such experiment can be confirmed as having taken place.

Ark Royal completed working up in January 1915, and on 1 February sailed to join the Allied fleet preparing to force a passage off the Dardanelles, arriving at the Aegean island of Tenedos on 17 February. She was to provide general aerial reconnaissance and, perhaps more importantly, spot gunfire against Turkish forts and forces ashore. This technique

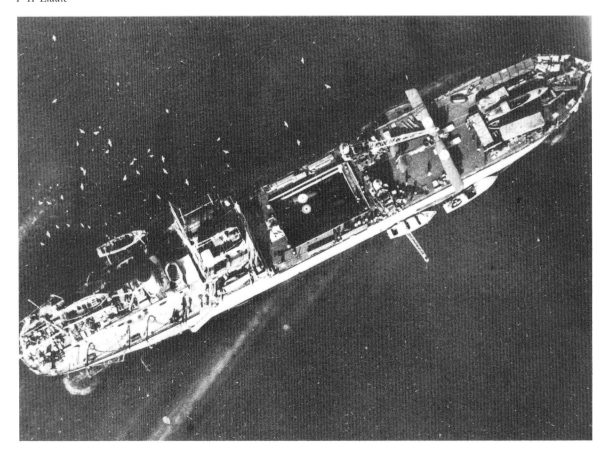

One of *Ark Royal*'s two Wight pushers, part of her original aerial complement, at the Dardanelles in 1915. One of the Wights made the first naval combat flight at the Dardanelles on 15 February 1915, scouting the straits, dropping a 20lb bomb on the Asiatic side and receiving seven bullet holes in return. *Ark Royal* is seen in the distance, alongside what may be the collier *Penmorvah*. *Author's collection*

did not work as well as had been hoped, largely because of inexperience and lack of preparation, but *Ark Royal* did give useful aerial support, her seaplanes replaced from time to time, before, during and after both the naval attempt to force passage of the straits and the subsequent land campaign on the Gallipoli peninsula.

This work continued until it became apparent that *Ark Royal*'s slow speed made her too much of a potential prey for German submarines, and she was replaced by *Ben-my-Chree* (qv). After taking part in a few subsidiary operations in the Aegean, she was stationed at Salonika as a seaplane depot ship from November 1915 to March 1916. In March she became a depot ship for the RNAS No 2 Wing (later the RAF 62nd and 63rd Wings), stationed at Mudros until April 1918 and after that at Syra until October.

After the armistice with Turkey, she served as an aircraft transport in the Black Sea and in December 1919 transported the personnel and twelve aircraft of Z Squadron, RAF, to British Somaliland for operations against native insurgents. In 1922–23, during the so-called Chanak Crisis, she was an aircraft transport and depot ship at the Dardanelles.

Various ancillary duties followed until 1930, when she was equipped with a catapult and performed valuably for the next few years as a catapult and seaplane trials and training vessel. On 21 December 1935, she was renamed *Pegasus* to clear the name *Ark Royal* for the flight-deck carrier that was to become famous in World War II.

After the start of that war in September 1939, *Pegasus* was used as an aircraft transport for the Home Fleet's Orkneys and Shetland Command until November, when she was designated the prototype Catapult Fighter Ship. She made three cruises as a convoy escort, carrying two or three Fairey Fulmar fighters, then was again used as a seaplane training ship until February 1944, when she was reduced to an accommodation vessel, a role lasting until May 1946. *Pegasus* was placed on the disposal list in June 1946 and purchased on 18 October for conversion to a merchantman to be named *Anita I*. The conversion was never completed and she was sold to a succession of shipbreakers, finally being scrapped at Grays, Essex, in 1950.

Aircraft operated by *Ark Royal* during World War I included Wight Pusher, Sopwith Types 807 and 860, Schneider and Baby, and Short Types 135, 166 and various models of Type 184. Sopwith Tabloid landplanes were originally embarked but were not used operationally by the ship. After the war, she transported de Havilland DH.9s and Bristol F.2Bs for the RAF and operated Fairey IIID floatplanes at the Dardanelles. As a catapult trials ship, she flung into the air a wide variety of aircraft, mostly obsolete RAF types. Subsequent aircraft included Fairey Swordfish, Supermarine Walrus and Fairey Fulmar.

Campania after her first conversion to an aviation vessel. *Imperial War Museum*

CAMPANIA

Displacement:	20,570t (20,900 tonnes), 12,950grt
Dimensions:	622ft oa × 65ft × 22ft – 28ft 5in (mean)
	(189m × 19.8m × 6.7m – 9.3m)
Machinery:	2 sets triple vertical expansion, 13 boilers, 2 shafts, 28,000–30,000ihp = 21.5–23.2kts (18kts in 1918)
	Coal: 3186t (3237.2 tonnes)
Armament:	6–4.7in (120mm) 6 × 1 LA, 1–3in/20cwt AA
Aircraft	
arrangements:	launching platform 165ft (50.3m) × ? in 1915, lengthened to 245ft (80.6m) × 44ft (14.4m) maximum in 1916; 1 forward hangar, 1 midships hangar; 2 derricks forward, 3 derricks midships, 1 derrick aft; 10–12 aircraft, 1 kite balloon after 1915
Complement:	(1918) 600 including 157 aviation personnel

Name	Builder	Laid down	Launched	Completed	Fate
CAMPANIA	Fairfield Shipbuilding & Engineering Company, Govan, Glasgow	?	8.9.1892	13.4.1893	Foundered 5.11.1918

Campania, built for the Cunard Company, held the Atlantic Blue Riband in 1893 and 1894 but in October 1914, worn from years of hard service and with her machinery in bad condition, she was sold to T W Ward for scrapping. Her breaking up was delayed pending an Admiralty decision on whether she should be acquired as an auxiliary cruiser, for, like other British liners of the period, she had been designed for this role as a wartime expedient and had been specially strengthened to mount eight 4.7in guns. This, in fact, did occur, but before much, if any, work had been done it was decided, upon the recommendation of Captain Murray Sueter, Director of the Air Department, to convert *Campania* into a seaplane carrier to

provide aerial reconnaissance for the Grand Fleet's Battle Fleet at Scapa Flow. It has been officially stated that she was chosen because she was the only immediately available ship large enough and speedy enough for the role, but that is difficult to accept, as other liners were, at that time, being transformed into auxiliary cruisers, transports or hospital ships. One can only guess that an aviation vessel simply ranked low in priority.

At any rate, *Campania* was purchased on 27 November 1914 and converted by Cammell, Laird & Company at Birkenhead, with a forward hangar and a launching platform over the forecastle sloping at an angle of 0°15′ from the bridge structure to the bow

Campania as she appeared after her second remodelling in 1915–16. The platform has been lengthened by running it between two split forefunnels and has a slightly greater angle, the mainmast has been moved forward and kite balloon facilities added at the stern. *Imperial War Museum*

Campania going down by the stern after collision damage in the Firth of Forth, 5 November 1918. *Photo by Melvin R Rattray, courtesy of the Rattray family*

(this structure prevented the planned mounting of a pair of 4.7in guns forward). She was commissioned on 17 April 1915, and joined the Battle Fleet at Scapa Flow, making her first operational cruise with that fleet on 11 June. Her defects quickly became apparent, but experiments in flying trolley-mounted Sopwith Schneiders off her platform in August and November proved the feasibility of the concept, and she was returned to Cammell, Laird in November for installation of a longer platform to permit takeoff by larger, wireless-equipped aircraft that would be of more use for reconnaissance.

The platform was lengthened by replacing the forward funnel with two side-by-side funnels through which the platform was extended, replacing the bridge with a jury structure. A second and larger hangar was added amidships, a well for a kite balloon was installed on the quarter deck, shielded by canvas wind-screens, as well as a hydrogen-generating plant and balloon winch, and a mounted anti-aircraft gun. The new platform sloped at about 4°.

Campania rejoined the Battle Fleet on 12 April 1916 with her Sopwiths supplemented by Short 184s. Her one chance for glory was aborted when she failed to receive the signal ordering the fleet to sortie for what became the Battle of Jutland. She sailed independently later, but was ordered to return because of the danger to an unescorted ship from submarines and also because of the mistaken belief that she lacked the speed to catch up with the fleet in a reasonable time.

Campania subseqently took part in some anti-submarine and anti-airship sweeps, but never got into action. Her value was increasingly eroded by her defective machinery, and well before the end of the war she was declared unfit for fleet duty although remaining with the fleet as a seaplane training and balloon depot ship. On 5 November 1918 she dragged her anchors during a gale in the Firth of Forth, colliding with battleship *Royal Oak* and, then, the large light cruiser *Glorious*; she foundered, fortunately with no loss of life.

Although *Campania* performed no operational service of any consequence, she contributed valuably to the development of deck flying. She had the distinction of being the first vessel ever referred to in an official communication as a 'fleet carrier', and also the first to have an aircraft named for her. This was the Fairey F.17 floatplane, called Campania because it was tailored to the dimensions of her hangar hatches, which measured 45ft (14.8m) × 20ft (6.5m) forward, 45ft (14.8m) × 30ft (9.8m) aft.

In addition to the F.17, she operated at various times the Sopwith Schneider, Baby, Pup and 1½ Strutter, and Short Type 184.

VINDEX

Displacement:	2950t (2997.4 tonnes), 1951grt
Dimensions:	361ft oa × 42ft × 13ft 3in (mean) (110m × 19.5m × 4m) 16ft 1in (max) (5.2m)
Machinery:	3 sets direct-drive turbines, 4 boilers, 3 shafts,11,000shp = 23kts 995 nm at 10kts. Coal: 475t (482 tonnes)
Armament:	2–12pdr/18cwt LA 2 × 1, increased to 4–12pdr/18cwt LA 4 × 1 and 1–6pdr AA (officially given as 2–6pdr AA but only one actually mounted)
Aircraft arrangements:	hangar aft, launching platform 64ft (19.5m) × 25ft (8.2m) maximum, 2 derricks forward, 2 cranes aft; 7 aircraft
Complement:	(1918) 218 including 76 aviation personnel

Name	Builder	Laid down	Launched	Completed	Fate
VINDEX, ex-VIKING	Armstrong, Whitworth & Company, Newcastle	1904	7.3.1905	26.6.1905	BU, 1954

Viking, a passenger vessel of the Isle of Man Steam Packet Company, was hired by the Admiralty on 26 March 1915 and purchased on 11 November, having, in the interim, been converted by the Cunard Company at Liverpool. She emerged as the first of what have since been called 'mixed carriers', with a hangar aft for five seaplanes and a launching platform forward for two aircraft with wheel undercarriage. The influence of the airship is seen strongly in *Vindex*, for her platform, like those of her successors, was intended not for flying-off of seaplanes on trolleys but for takeoff by landplanes for airship interception. In *Vindex*, these were originally Bristol Scout C models armed with explosive darts.

Commissioned under her new name in November 1915, *Vindex* was assigned to the Harwich Force that month and was active in the North Sea and in operations against the German coast until 1917, also based in the Nore for anti-airship patrols. In the first interception of an airship by a carrier-based aeroplane, one of her Bristols unsuccessfully attacked Zeppelin L.17 on 2 August 1916.

In 1918, she was transferred to the Mediterranean, where she served until she was sold back to her owner on 12 February 1920, and reverted to her original name. Requisitioned again in 1939 for use as a

Vindex, first of the so-called mixed carriers, with launching platform forward and seaplane hangar aft. *Fleet Air Arm Museum*

Vindex at sea in May 1916 during an unsuccessful attempt to attack the German airship base at Tondern. A Sopwith Baby is being hoisted aft and a Bristol Scout is on the forward platform. *J M Bruce/G S Leslie collection*

troopship, she was returned to her owner in 1945 and sold for scrapping in 1954.

Her 1915–20 aircraft included Bristol Scouts C and D, Short 184, and Sopwith Schneider, Baby and $1\frac{1}{2}$ Strutter.

Vindex had the distinction of being the first RN vessel of any type to fly off a landplane, a flight made on 3 November 1915 by Flight Lieutenant B F Fowler (not Towler as often stated) in a Bristol Scout C.

MANXMAN

Displacement:	3090t (3139.6 tonnes), 2048grt
Dimensions:	334ft pp × 43ft 1in × 14ft 3in (mean)
	(109.8m × 14.1m × 4.7m)
Machinery:	3 sets direct-drive turbines, 3 boilers, 3 shafts, 6300shp = 18kt. Coal: 430t (437 tonnes)
Armament:	2–12pdr/18cwt LA 2 × 1, 1–6pdr AA, increased to 4–12pdr/18cwt LA 4 × 1 and 2-6pdr AA
Aircraft arrangements:	hangar aft, launching platform 86ft (28.2m) × 28ft (9.2m) maximum; fore-and-aft gantry and 2 jib cranes aft, 2 derricks forward; 8 aircraft (4 seaplanes aft, 4 landplanes forward)
Complement:	(1918) 223 including 73 aviation personnel

Name	Builder	Laid down	Launched	Completed	Fate
MANXMAN	Vickers Sons & Maxim, Barrow-in-Furness	?	15.6.1904	1904	BU, 1949

Purchased by the Admiralty from Midland Railway Company on 17 April 1916, this Isle of Man packet was converted at Chatham Dockyard, and commissioned in December 1916 as the second of the so-called mixed carriers. She was the first British carrier to operate the Sopwith Pup.

Manxman was attached to the Battle Cruiser Force at Rosyth and supported North Sea minelaying operations during April–July 1917. She was far from the ideal aviation vessel for this force, for her horsepower and speed had fallen off drastically from the 8500shp and 22.5kts she had attained during trials in 1904. She was transferred in October 1917 to the Mediterranean, where she served for the rest of the war, based at Syracuse, Taranto and Brindisi. In January 1918 she made a dash to Mudros for an unsuccessful attempt to attack the German battle cruiser *Goeben* aground in the Dardanelles after her sortie of that month.

Manxman was sold to the Isle of Man Steam Packet Company on 12 February 1920. She was requisitioned by the Admiralty in October 1941 for conversion to a radar training ship, renamed *Caduceus*, and scrapped in 1949.

Manxman, second of the mixed carriers. She introduced the Sopwith Pup into British shipboard aviation. *Imperial War Museum*

Nairana, with a Sopwith Pup or Beardmore WB.III on the platform and the empennage of a Short 184 protruding from the hangar. *Photo by Melvin H Rattray, courtesy of the Rattray family*

Nairana at sea, wearing the dazzle colours sported by the carriers late in the war. This view shows the placement of the armament. *Courtesy of P E Maitland*

NAIRANA

Displacement:	3070t (3119 tonnes)
Dimensions:	352ft oa × 45ft 6in × 13ft 2in (mean) (107.3m × 14m × 4.2m) 13ft 10in (max) (4.3m)
Machinery:	2 sets geared turbines, 6 boilers, 2 shafts, 6700shp = 19kts (7003shp = 20.32kts on trials) Coal: 448t (455.2 tonnes)
Armament:	2–12pdr/18cwt LA 2 × 1, 2–12pdr AA 2 × 1
Aircraft arrangements:	aft hangar, launching platform 94ft (28.9m) × 23ft (7.5m) maximum; fore-and-aft gantry aft, 2 derricks forward; 7–8 aircraft
Complement:	(1918) 278 including 90 aviation personnel

Name	Builder	Laid down	Launched	Completed	Fate
NAIRANA	William Denny & Bros, Dumbarton	?	?	25.8.1917	BU, 1951

Nairana was under construction for the Australian firm of Huddart, Parker Ltd when hired on the stocks for conversion to the mixed carrier configuration. She was attached to the Battle Cruiser Force at Rosyth in August 1917 soon after commissioning but saw little action, being employed mainly for training pilots in deck takeoffs and ferrying aircraft to warships equipped with launching platforms.

She served briefly in the Mediterranean in 1918, and in mid-1919 took part in the British intervention at Archangel. She was sold to Tasmanian Steamers Pty in 1920, and remodelled for mercantile use. She ran aground at Port Melbourne on 18 February 1951 and was subsequently scrapped.

Aircraft operated by *Nairana* were Short Type 184, Beardmore W B III, Sopwith 2F.1 Camel and, at Archangel, Fairey Campania.

Pegasus, last of the mixed carriers, in late 1918.
*Photo by Melvin H Rattray, courtesy of the
Rattray family*

Pegasus in the Firth of Forth, 4 October 1918, with two Sopwith 2F.1 Camels on her platform. This photo and the preceding one show how the dazzle pattern differed on port and starboard. *Courtesy of P H Liddle*

PEGASUS

Displacement:	3300t (3353 tonnes)
Dimensions:	332ft oa × 43ft × 15ft 4in (mean)
	(102m × 13.1m × 4.6m)
Machinery:	2 sets geared turbines, ? boilers, 2 shafts, 9700shp = 20.25kts (9704shp = 20.8kts on trials).
	Oil: 360t (365.7 tonnes)
Armament:	2–12pdr LA 2 × 1, 2–12pdr AA 2 × 1
Aircraft arrangements:	hangar aft, launching platform 82ft (25m) × 28ft (9.5m) maximum; 2 jib cranes aft, 2 derricks forward; 9 aircraft
Complement:	(1918) 258 including 100 aviation personnel

Name	Builder	Laid down	Launched	Completed (commissioned)	Fate
PEGASUS, ex-STOCKHOLM	John Brown & Company, Clydebank	?	9.6.1917	28.8.1917	BU, 1931

Pegasus alongside battle cruiser *Repulse* in March 1918. A Sopwith 2F.1 Camel is on *Repulse*'s B turret aircraft platform and another is aboard *Pegasus*. The carrier was frequently used to ferry aircraft to capital ships. *Author's collection*

As the mercantile *Stockholm*, this vessel was under construction for the Great Eastern Railway when purchased on 27 February 1917 for completion as a carrier. Her commissioning three days after *Nairana*'s made her marginally the last of the mixed carriers, with five fighters carried forward and four seaplanes aft. She was also probably the best laid-out and most efficient of the four, as witnessed by the fact she was the only one retained after the war.

Pegasus served with the Grand Fleet at Rosyth during 1917–18. She took part in a few uneventful North Sea operations with the Battle Cruiser Force but, like *Nairana*, was employed mostly in pilot training and ferrying aircraft to platform-equipped capital ships.

She was stationed at Archangel from May to September 1919 during the British intervention here and served at the Dardanelles in 1920 during the Chanak Crisis. She was attached to the Mediterranean Fleet from 1920 to 1924, with the lanching platform removed in 1923, and rerated as an aircraft tender in 1924. After special service at Singapore in 1924–25, she was placed in reserve at Devonport on 5 July 1925. *Pegasus* was briefly recommissioned in 1929 and sold for scrapping at Morecambe on 22 August 1931.

Aircraft operated by *Pegasus* included Sopwith 2F.1 Camel, Beardmore W B III, Short Type 184, Fairey Campania, Fairey IIIC (at Archangel and the Dardanelles) and Fairey IIID.

BROCKLESBY, KILLINGHOLME

Displacement:	508grt
Dimensions:	195ft × 31ft 1in × 8ft 7in
	(59.4m × 9.5m × 2.5m)
Machinery:	2 sets 2-cylinder compound diagonal engines, 2 paddlewheels

No other particulars recorded

Name	Builder	Laid down	Launched	Completed	Fate
BROCKLESBY	Earle's Shipbuilding & Engineering Company, Hull	?	?	1912	BU, 1936
KILLINGHOLME					BU, 1945

These two vessels were together with the French pair described earlier the only paddle steamers to carry aircraft operationally during World War I. Double ender sidewheelers, they were built for the Great Central Railway's ferry service between Hull and New Holland on the River Humber. They were taken over by the Royal Navy on 21 February 1916 to carry two

Killingholme in prewar colours, not long after her completion in 1912. *Author's collection*

or three Sopwith Schneider or Baby floatplanes for coastal anti-airship patrol, rated as fleet messengers.

Killingholme, which was damaged by a mine in 1916, was based at Killingholme and *Brocklesby* at Yarmouth. Their few attempts at airship interception were totally unsuccessful, and they were paid off in 1917 – *Killingholme* on 21 April and *Brocklesby* on 9 June – for return to their owner.

Ownership of both was transferred to the London & Great Eastern Railway Company when it took

Killingholme, with a Sopwith Baby aboard,
showing mine damage sustained in 1916. It was
believed at the time, in a story widely repeated,
that she had been struck by a torpedo from a
disguised German trawler. *Imperial War Museum*

over Great Central Railway in 1923 and both were
employed in excursion cruising. *Brocklesby* was sold
to Redcliffe Shipping Company in February 1935 and
renamed *Highland Queen*, but was scrapped the next
year. *Killingholme* was requisitioned by the Admiralty
in May 1941 for use as a barrage balloon vessel at

Grimsby. Returned to her owner in March 1945, she
was scrapped without re-entering service.

Two trawlers, the 322-ton *Kingfisher* and the 302-
ton *Cantarice*, were similarly equipped to carry Schneiders for anti-airship patrol in the North Sea. They
were equally unsuccessful, and *Cantarice* was sunk by
a mine in November 1916.

The auxiliary cruisers *Laconia* and *Himalaya* each
operated a Short Type 827 floatplane in operations
off the East African coast in 1916, with temporary
canvas hangars, but neither can be considered an
aviation vessel.

FURIOUS

Displacement:	19,100t (19,407 tonnes) normal, 22,405t (22,765 tonnes) full load (published figures on *Furious'* displacement vary, probably because it did actually vary, as weight was added and substracted during remodellings)
Dimensions:	786ft 3in oa × 88ft (over bulges) × 21ft 6in (mean) (239.7m × 26.8m × 6.85m) 25ft (max) (7.6m)
Machinery:	2 sets geared turbines, 18 boilers, 4 shafts, 90,000shp (90,825shp on trials) = 31.5kts. 6000 nm at 20kts, 11,000 nm at 'economical speed'. Oil: 3400t (3454 tonnes)
Armament:	(as completed) 1–18in (457mm) (2–18in as designed). 11–5.5in (138.6mm) LA 11 × 1, 2–3in (76.2mm) AA 2 × 1, 4–3pdr 4 × 1, 18–21in (533mm) TT 4 × 3, 2 × 2, 2 single submerged. After March 1918: 10–5.5in (138.6mm) LA 10 × 1, 5–3in (76.2mm) AA 5 × 1, 4–3pdr 4 × 1, 5 MG (1 landing). 12–21in (533mm) TT 4 × 3
Armour:	(as completed) belt 2–3in (15–76.2mm), deck 1–3in (25–76.2mm), barbette 3–7in (76.2–177.4mm), turret 5–9in (127–229mm), conning tower 10in (254mm)

continued over page

(HMS Furious continued)

**Aircraft
arrangements:** (as completed) forward hangar 64ft (21m) × 36ft (11.8m), forward takeoff deck 228ft (69.5m) × 50ft (15.2m) with collapsible wind-breaks port and starboard, slot-mounted trolley on takeoff deck for launching seaplanes, 2 derricks forward. After March 1918: as above with addition of aft hangar 70ft (23m) × 38ft (12.5m), aft landing deck 284ft (86.5m) × 70ft (23m), electrically powered lifts 48ft (15.7m) × 18ft (5.9m) fore and aft

Complement: (1917) 880 including 84 aviation personnel; (1918) 932 including 175 aviation personnel

Name	Builder	Laid down	Launched	Completed	Fate
FURIOUS	Armstrong, Whitworth & Company, Newcastle	8.6.1915	18.8.1916	26.6.1917	BU, 1948

Furious was the third of Lord Fisher's infamous 'large light cruisers', designed to support his so-called Baltic Project troop landings on the German Pomeranian coast, all eventually destined to become flight-deck carriers.

Furious started down this road in March 1917 upon recommendation of the Grand Fleet Aircraft Committee that she be altered to a 'fast seaplane carrier' with a flight platform replacing the forward 18in gun. She joined the Battle Fleet on 4 July 1917 with an original air complement of five Sopwith Pups and three Short Type 184 seaplanes. The first deck landing upon a moving ship was accomplished aboard her on 2 August 1917 by Squadron Commander E H Dunning in a Pup. He repeated the feat on 7 August but was killed in a second attempt that day.

Operations in the North Sea during September–November 1917 led the Grand Fleet Aircraft Committee to recommend that *Furious* be altered to provide a means of recovering aircraft directly aboard in a less risky manner, and on 14 November 1917 she was detached for modifications by Armstrong, Whitworth. These included removal of the 18in gun and mainmast and their replacement with an aft

Furious, as completed with 18in gun aft, off the British coast 3 September 1917. A Short seaplane is on the forward deck. *Graham Mottram collection*

hangar and landing deck, installation of lifts fore and aft (the aft one displaced to starboard), removal of one 5.5in gun and redistribution of the remaining ten guns, and an increase in anti-aircraft armament. In addition, the forward and aft aircraft decks were connected by port and starboard gangways measuring 170ft (55.9m) × 11ft (3.6m). The aircraft complement was increased from a nominal ten to a nominal sixteen.

Furious was recommissioned at Rosyth on 15 March 1918 as a flagship, Admiral Commanding Aircraft, Grand Fleet, with Sopwith 1½ Strutter landplanes replacing the seaplanes. Landing experiments with Pups with their wheel undercarriage replaced by skids began in April. For these, an arresting system, which had been tested on land, was installed. This consisted of fore-and-aft wires, raised slightly above deck by wooden pegs, that were engaged by hooks in the Pups' skids. A system of athwartship wires weighted by sandbags, very similar to that installed on the US

A Sopwith Pup fitted with skids landing on
Furious, early 1918. The vertical cables of the
primitive crash barrier are prominent in the
foreground. It is possible that this was one of
the few successful landings. *Imperial War
Museum*

Furious in her second configuration as a carrier,
with landing deck aft. Wind-breaking palisades
are up on her forward deck and three aircraft,
two with wings folded, are ranged around the
open forward lift. *Courtesy of P E Maitland*

Two Sopwith Pups on the forward deck of
Furious. Wind-breaking palisades have been
raised. The four-wheel slot-fitted trolley for
launching seaplanes is visible in the foreground.
Real Photographs

A broadside view of *Furious* in her second stage.
Airship NS.7 is approaching, apparently for a
deck landing experiment. *J M Bruce/G S Leslie
collection*

cruiser *Pennsylvania* (qv) seven years earlier, was tried briefly but abandoned as impractical. As a safety measure, a crash barrier consisting of cables strung vertically from a gantry-like frame was installed just abaft the funnel.

Use of the landing deck, however, proved practically impossible in the face of draughts and eddies of air and gases streaming from the centreline superstructure and funnel. Of thirteen attempts, only three were successful; in the others, the Pups were wrecked or damaged, breaking up on deck, hitting the crash barrier or going over the side.

Use of the landing deck was subsequently abandoned, but *Furious* took part in fleet operations from

Airship SSZ.59 aboard *Furious*'s aft deck after a successful landing experiment in 1918. *Courtesy of P E Maitland*

A stern view of *Furious* displays the dazzle colours she wore in late 1918. *Author's collection*

June to November 1918, the Pups replaced by W B IIIs and later by Sopwith 2F.1 Camels. On 19 June two of the Camels shot down a German seaplane, and on 7 July *Furious* flew off seven Camels for an attack on the airship base at Tondern that destroyed Zeppelins L.54 and L.60 in the most successful exploit by shipboard aviation during the entire war.

After the war, *Furious* was attached to the Atlantic Fleet for twelve months and took part briefly in operations in the Baltic before being placed in reserve on 21 November 1919. She was reconstructed into a flight-deck carrier at Devonport Dockyard during 1922–25 and received major structural modifications in 1930–31 and 1938–39. After long, arduous and

varied service in World War II she was so worn, with some major structural parts irreplaceable, that she was reduced to reserve on 15 September 1944. She was used after the war as a target ship for tests of explosives and sold for scrapping in 1948.

In addition to the aircraft noted above, *Furious* operated one or more Sopwith Babys and postwar is believed to have embarked briefly Sopwith Cuckoo torpedo planes. In 1918 two experimental and successful landings of small naval airships were made on her aft deck.

VINDICTIVE

Displacement:	9344t (9494 tonnes) light, 9750t (9906.7 tonnes) standard, 12,100t (12,294 tonnes) normal, 12,400t (12,599 tonnes) full load
Dimensions:	605ft oa × 65ft 2in × 17ft 6in (mean) (184.4m × 21.4m × 5.7m) 20ft 6in (maximum) (6.7m)
Machinery:	4 scts geared turbines, 12 boilers, 4 shafts, 60,000shp − 29.75−28kts (63,600shp = 29.12kts on trials) 3000 nm at 23−24kts, 5400 nm at 14kts. Coal: 860t (873.8 tonnes). Oil: 1480t (1503 tonnes)
Armament:	4−7.5in/45 (189.9mm) LA 4 × 1, 4−3in (76.2mm) LA 4 × 1, 4−3in (76.2mm) AA 4 × 1, 4 MG, 6−21in (533mm) TT 6 × 1
Armour:	belt 1½−3in (38−76.2mm), deck 1−1½in (25−38mm), conning tower 3in (76.2mm), gun shields 1in (25mm)
Aircraft arrangements:	(as completed) forward hangar 78ft (25.6m) × 49ft (16.1m) aft tapering to 44ft (14.4m) forward, forward flight platform 106ft (32.4m) × 49ft (16.1m) maximum, aft landing platform 193ft (58.8m) × 57ft (17.3m), 2 derricks forward, 1 derrick aft; 6−12 aircraft
Complement:	(1918) 648 including 71 aviation personnel

Name	Builder	Laid down	Launched	Completed	Fate
VINDICTIVE, ex-CAVENDISH	Harland & Wolff Ltd, Belfast	29.6.1916	17.1.1918	21.9.1918	BU, 1946

Vindictive during Baltic operations in 1919, seaplanes with folded wings on her aft deck. *Courtesy of Eric Harlin via Ian M Burns*

This vessel was ordered as *Cavendish* in April 1916 as the first of the five-ship improved *Birmingham* class (also known as the *Cavendish*, *Hawkins* or *Raleigh* class). The first large cruisers ordered by the Royal Navy in a decade, they were intended to cope with German surface commerce raiders. Their size and armament, as well as the RN insistence upon retaining them, were influential factors in determining the upper limits of cruisers set forth in the Washington Naval Treaty.

The need for another fast carrier for the Grand Fleet caused *Cavendish*'s design to be altered during construction. She emerged as a pocket *Furious* with a takeoff deck forward and a landing deck aft, renamed *Vindictive* in honour of the old cruiser that had performed so valiantly during the Zeebrugge Raid.

The aircraft arrangements necessitated a reduction in the main battery, from seven guns to four. The takeoff platform formed the roof of the hangar, and had the same dimensions with a 28ft (9.2m) extension, which brought the total length to 106ft (32.4m). A hatch at the aft end gave access to the hangar, but

Vindictive aground near Reval, July 1919, shortly after entering the Baltic. *Courtesy of Eric Harlin via Ian M Burns*

Another view of *Vindictive* aground shows details of her forward take-off deck, with wind-breaking palisades raised. *Courtesy of Eric Harlin via Ian M Burns*

A view of *Vindictive*'s aft hangar and landing deck. *Courtesy of Eric Harlin via Ian M Burns*

A Sopwith Pup flown by W W Wakefield approaching *Vindictive* on 1 November 1919 for the first and only landing made on her deck. *Courtesy of D K Brown*

no lift was provided. Port and starboard gangways connected the aircraft decks, permitting, as in *Furious*, transfer of folded-wing aircraft between them.

After commissioning on 1 October 1918 *Vindictive* joined the Grand Fleet's Flying Squadron, as its carrier division was called, on 18 October but was too late to see operational service. Instead, she spent

the next few months carrying out aircraft experiments and exercises, including the first shipboard trials of the Grain Griffin, two of which were lost in accidents. On 1 November the first and only landing was made on her aft deck by W W Wakefield (later Lord Wakefield of Kendal) in the fleet's last operational Sopwith Pup.

On 2 July 1919, *Vindictive* sailed to join the British naval force operating against the Bolsheviks in the Baltic; she carried twelve aircraft, a mixture of Sopwith

Vindictive recovering a Grain Griffin, one of two aircraft of this type involved in accidents during deck flying exercises. *Courtesy of Eric Harlin via Ian M Burns*

Short 184s aboard *Vindictive* in the Baltic in 1919. The view shows how the 63½ft wingspan of the 184 could be reduced by folding for handier shipboard accommodation. *Courtesy of Eric Harlin via Ian M Burns*

2F.1 Camels, Sopwith 1½ Strutters, Short 184s and Grain Griffins. She grounded near Reval on 6 July and was refloated with great difficulty after eight days. Subsequently, she served in the Baltic, save for one brief return to home waters, during late December. Her aircraft were extremely active during this period, flying scores of bombing, reconnaissance and gunfire-spotting missions, but, except for a bombing raid on Kronstadt on 30 July, they operated from shore and harbour bases. For that operation, in which twelve aircraft took part, the forward platform was given a temporary extension to 118ft (38.8m) to provide a longer takeoff run. On the same day as that raid, *Vindictive* took on duty as a depot ship for eight coastal motor boats (motor torpedo boats).

She left the Baltic with the rest of the British force on 22 December 1919 and was paid off at Portsmouth on 24 December. From February 1920, she was alternately in reserve and on duty as a troop transport until paying off at Chatham on 1 March 1923 for reconversion to a cruiser. All the aircraft structures except the hangar were removed; two 7.5in guns were added; the 3in AA reduced to three and rearranged. She retained her aviation association, however, for a Carey catapult was mounted atop the hangar, the first to be carried by a conventional British warship. As there was still no lift, a starboard crane replaced the forward derricks for aircraft handling.

The first catapult launch of a standard British naval aircraft, a Fairey IIID floatplane, was made by *Vindictive* on 3 October 1925. The vessel also carried out catapult trials of float-equipped Fairey Flycatcher fighters.

On 1 January 1926, carrying six IIIDs, *Vindictive* sailed for the China Station, where she served until 14 March 1928, operating these aircraft and on occasion Flycatchers for anti-piracy patrol and to help quell civil disturbances. She returned to home waters in May 1928, and the catapult was removed at Chatham in August, ending her career as an aviation vessel.

Another spell in reserve and as a personnel transport ensued until in May 1937 she was demilitarized under terms of the London Navy Treaty and converted to a cadet training ship, commissioning in this role on 7 September. The outbreak of war put an end to this service, and she was converted again – this time to a repair ship, commissioning in February 1940 with the hangar finally removed. *Vindictive* took part in operations off Norway and then until August 1945 served in the South Atlantic and Mediterranean and with the Home Fleet. Reduced to reserve on 8 September 1945, she was sold for scrapping on 24 January 1946, and broken up later that year at Blyth.

ARGUS

Displacement:	15,775t (16,128.5 tonnes) normal, 14,450t (14,682 tonnes) standard, 16,500t (16,754 tonnes) full load
Dimensions:	565ft oa × 68ft × 21ft (mean)
	(172.2m × 20.7m × 6.4m)
Machinery:	2 sets geared turbines, 12 boilers, 4 shafts, 21,376shp = 20.5kts. 4370 nm at 16kts. Oil: 2000t (2032.1 tonnes)
Armament:	2–4in (101.2mm) LA 2 × 1, 2–4in (101.2mm) AA 2 × 1 as designed, 2–4in LA, 4–4in AA as completed
Aircraft arrangements:	flight deck 550ft (167.6m) × 68ft (20.7m) maximum, hangar 350ft (106.6m) × 68ft (20.7m) maximum, forward lift 30ft (9.1m) × 36ft (10.9m), aft lift 60ft (18.2m) × 18ft (5.4m), 2 derricks forward, 2 cranes aft; 20–21 aircraft
Complement:	(1918) 495 including 180 aviation personnel

Name	Builder	Laid down	Launched	Completed (commissioned)	Fate
ARGUS, ex-CONTE ROSSO	William Beardmore & Company, Dalmuir	June 1914	2.12.1917	14.9.1918	BU, 1946

Argus began life as one of two cargo-liners ordered in 1914 by the Italian Lloyd Sabaudo Line, to be named *Conte Rosso*. Work upon both ceased at the outbreak of war.

The chain of events that led to transformation of *Conte Rosso* into *Argus*, the world's first flight-deck carrier, started with a request to the Board of Admiralty in May 1916 from Admiral Sir John Jellicoe, Grand Fleet commander, that a special aviation ship be laid down to replace or supplement the collection of mercantile conversions he had been given to protect his fleet from the prying eyes of German airships. By this time, deck flying had been proved possible and practical, and the board was prepared to give serious consideration to the request, with the result that, in August, it decided to acquire the two incomplete Italian vessels for redesign as aviation ships. They possessed adequate dimensions and, being already in frame, could be completed more quickly than a vessel built from the keel. However, reportedly owing to the more pressing need for other types of naval construction, it was decided the next month to proceed with only one of them.

The original design of *Argus* is attributed to Lieutenant R A Holmes RNVR, a former assistant naval architect for the Cunard Company who had served in *Riviera* since her first conversion. The previous year, he had drawn up plans for what was called a

A model of the original design of *Argus*, as wind-tunnel tested at the National Physical Laboratory. *Courtesy of D K Brown*

'seaplane-carrying cruiser' that featured a slipway at the stern for aircraft recovery. Strong doubt was expressed about the feasibility of this idea, and nothing further came of the design.

For *Argus*, Holmes proposed a flat, unobstructed deck from which wheeled aircraft could operate. It was to be clear of any form of superstructure, and engine room smoke and gases, instead of being carried away in normal funnels, were to be dispelled through two long horizontal ducts, one on each side of the ship, discharging at the stern.

At this point, the Admiralty construction department took matters over, and the principal designer of *Argus* was J H Narbeth, Assistant Director of Naval Construction. Whether he or others were responsible for alteration of the Holmes' concept is unclear, but what emerged was rather a combination of the 1912 Beardmore plan and a quasi-*Campania*, with a takeoff

Argus as completed, with flush deck, wearing the dazzle paint scheme of her brief wartime career. *Courtesy of Eric J Penny*

Argus with dummy island superstructure fitted for
landing experiments in early October 1918.
Author's collection

deck forward and a landing deck aft, separated by
parallel deckhouses port and starboard connnected
by an athwartships navigating bridge. Holmes' 'tunnel
funnels' were retained, running along each side of
what would have been the shelter deck in the mercantile design and now became a hangar deck. The hangar
itself was 330ft (108.5m) × 68ft (20.7m) narrowing to
48ft (15.7m). The hangar deck was to be the strength
deck; it was to be roofed, with a light flight deck, fitted
with expansion joints, carried 14ft 6in (4.8m) above

the roof on a steel web framework, leaving an open
space between. Aft of the superstructure, the landing
deck was to measure approximately 300ft (98.7m) × 68 ft
(20.7m). The takeoff deck, probably more properly
described as a platform, was considerably narrower
and extended on a trestle-like structure about 200ft
(98.7m) to the bow. Hangar and flight decks were
connected by two lifts, one forward, one aft, of the
same dimensions actually fitted on *Argus* (although a
photograph of a model of the proposed design shows

A closeup view of the dummy island on *Argus*.
The forward lift is in the down position. *Courtesy*
of Eric Harlin via Ian M Burns

what appear to be two lifts forward).

Narbeth evidently liked Holmes' plan for a stern slipway for seaplane recovery and reportedly spent some time trying to graft such a feature onto the ship before the idea was abandoned. Instead, seaplanes were to be handled by four cranes, one forward and one aft of the deckhouses on each side. A crash barrier similar to that later installed on *Furious* was to be strung between the two pieces of superstructure.

There would appear to have been some initial confusion about what role the ship was supposed to play; two separate sets of aircraft complements were originally proposed. One would have consisted entirely of floatplanes – four Shorts, six Sopwith Babys and eight AD Navyplanes. The AD (Air Department) Navyplane was a two-place, twin-float pusher-engine biplane. Seven were ordered in 1916 but only one was built and it was not a success. Apparently *Argus*' designers placed great faith in it. The alternative was 20 Sopwith T.1 Cuckoo torpedo planes, single-seat biplanes with wheel undercarriage, of the type that *Argus* eventually did embark.

Argus had either been launched or was near launching, with portions of the superstructure in place, when results of wind-tunnel tests of a model of the configuration at the National Physical Laboratory at Teddington in November 1916 showed that these protuberances created highly adverse air flow, so well before the landing experiments on *Furious* confirmed the problem, it was back to the drawing board for *Argus*. The difficulty now was how to obtain an unobstructed deck and still allow the ship to be conned and navigated in the absence of normal superstructure.

A solution had been proposed earlier by an RNAS aviator, Flight Commander Hugh A Williamson, who served aboard *Ark Royal* in the Dardanelles, and had been assigned to the Air Department's design section after a crash there. His plan was to move the entire superstructure – bridge, funnels, masts, etc – to one side of a ship, leaving a deck unobstructed from bow to stern and equally clear over two-thirds or so of the breadth; in short, an island of the kind that in one form or another has been on nearly every aircraft carrier to this day.

Williamson carved a crude model of such a craft, and in September 1915 presented it and the idea to Narbeth, who at once realized that there would be a problem with weight distribution when normally centerline funnel uptakes were canted to one side. After consideration, however, he thought the difficulty could be solved, and he was indeed to overcome it in the next war-designed carrier, *Eagle*. Williamson's proposed ship, which also featured a rather impractical arresting system, formed of upward sloping wires, was discussed by the Admiralty Seaplane Committee later in 1915 but the idea went no further at that time.

A Sopwith 1½ Strutter landing on *Argus* during tests to determine the effects of the dummy island on flight operations. *J M Bruce/G S Leslie collection*

The island idea was broached again during discussions of *Argus*' redesign, although not by Williamson, who took no part in these consultations. But it lost out to the original plan for a completely clear deck. Instead of an island, *Argus* was fitted with a hydraulically retractable pilothouse-charthouse that was lowered flush with the flight deck during flying operations.

The 'tunnel funnels' were further refined to cope with the expected problem of interior overheating once the plan of leaving open space between hangar and flight decks was abandoned. The long ducts, of oval section, measuring 14ft 3in (4.7m) × 8ft (2.6m) internally, were surrounded by outer casings of 15ft 9in (5.2m) × 9ft 6in (3.1m) through which cooling air was driven by fans. In service, however, overheating did occur. The ducts themselves were fitted with fans to draw out smoke and gases, as well as smoke-suppression apparatus.

Because of the time lost in redesign, *Argus*, after commissioning at Dalmuir on 14 September 1918 and joining the Grand Fleet at the Firth of Forth, was too late to see operational service. The first landings on and takeoffs from her deck were made on 24 Sep-

Argus postwar in the configuration in which she would be most recognized and remembered. The retractable pilot house and masts are raised. *J M Bruce/G S Leslie collection*

Argus rigged for flight operations, with the pilot house retracted. *Courtesy of Bruce Robertson*

tember by RAF Lieutenant Colonel (later RN Vice Admiral) Richard Bell Davies, VC, and Captain L H Cockey, flying Sopwith 1½ Strutters. Two days later, twenty-one landings and takeoffs were made.

Meanwhile, Narbeth had been considering an island superstructure for *Eagle*. Wind-tunnel tests of a model indicated that the air flow around such a structure would not impede aerial operations, but more practical and realistic experience was desired. Consequently, a large wood-and-canvas dummy island was erected on *Argus*' starboard side in early October. Several successful landings and takeoffs were made with it in place, and *Eagle* was subsequently completed with an island.

In later years, Williamson came to believe that the

A Sopwith 1½ Strutter making an awkward landing on *Argus*, possibly in October 1918. It is fitted with a hydrovane, to help prevent noseover in a water touchdown, and a hook on the landing gear axle to engage fore-and-aft arresting lines on the carrier's deck. *Courtesy of Eric J Penny*

A Sopwith T.1 Cuckoo with torpedo mounted. This is probably one of the torpedo planes embarked by *Argus* in October 1918 for a proposed attack on the German fleet. *Courtesy of Eric J Penny*

starboard placement of *Argus'* dummy island and *Eagle*'s real one resulted from a similar positioning of the island on his 1915 model – which, he said, was arbitrary although one might suspect he had been unconsciously influenced by the right-hand driver's position in British motor vehicles. Narbeth, however, is said to have chosen that position because several pilots had said that should they fail to make a deck landing on the first attempt, they would turn to the left to clear the ship. This preference can be attributed to the influence of the rotary engines that powered the Sopwith aircraft most frequently used in British deck landing experiments. In a rotary, the entire engine revolved rapidly around a fixed crankshaft, which imparted a gyroscopic-torque effect, tending strongly to nose an aeroplane down in a right turn and up in a left turn.

The dummy island was removed from *Argus* immediately after these tests, and during October 10–19 she embarked the personnel and aircraft of a squadron of Sopwith T.1 Cuckoo torpedo planes intended for an attack on the German fleet at Wilhelmshaven. By the time their pilots had gained enough experience to operate from the carrier, the

armistice had occurred.

The first landings on *Argus* were made on a bare deck but she was soon equipped with a system of fore-and-aft wires, similar to that installed on *Furious*, which were engaged by hooks on the aircraft's landing gear axle. The resulting friction had a braking effect, but the purpose was less to prevent overshooting the deck than to keep the aircraft from veering to the side, which tended to occur when rudder control was diminished upon landing. Variations of this system were tried out, including one in which one of the lifts was lowered slightly to form an aircraft 'trap'. None of these was really satisfactory, and for a time there was a return to bare-deck landings on British carriers until finally an athwartship arresting system along American lines was developed.

Argus' first operational service came in July 1919, when she transported Fairey IIIC floatplanes to *Pegasus* at Archangel. For the next couple of years she served alternately in the Atlantic and the Mediterranean, involved mainly in deck trials of varied types of aircraft, including an unsuccessful attempt on 31 August 1922 to launch a remote-control drone, the Royal Aircraft Establishment 1921 Target. She was stationed at the Dardanelles during the Chanak Crisis in September and October 1922, on 11 October flying off to a landing field twelve Bristol F.2B fighters she had embarked from *Ark Royal*.

Argus served in the Atlantic, Mediterranean and the China Station until going into reserve on 7 May 1930 at Portsmouth. She was recommissioned on 28 May 1938 as a deck-landing training ship and was also fitted with a catapult to operate wireless-controlled de Havilland Queen Bee anti-aircraft target planes. Only a few of these, however, were actually flown from her.

Argus was undergoing a refit when war erupted, and she was recommissioned on 5 November 1939 for service in the Mediterranean as a deck-landing training ship. She continued in this role, and as an aircraft transport, for the next four years, although such was the need for carriers that she was frequently pressed into more active service. She ferried fighters to Malta several times and once to Murmansk. In November 1942, her aircraft helped fly cover for the Operation Torch landings in North Africa and on 10 November she was damaged by a German dive bomber, which killed four men.

The veteran ship's services finally came to an end on 21 October 1944 when she paid off at Gillingham. The last aircraft to rise from her deck had been a Fairey Swordfish on 24 September.

As the world's first flight-deck carrier, *Argus* had a remarkable and varied career and rendered far more valuable wartime service than her American and Japanese near-contemporaries, *Langley* and *Hosho*. During her time, she carried and flew off, either experimentally, operationally or in ferrying service, at least 44 different types of aircraft – probably a record for any carrier of any nationality. They are worth listing in full (the order is alphabetical):

Auster III, Avro Bison and 504N, Blackburn Blackburn, Dart and Skua, Bristol F.2B, de Havilland DH.9, DH.9A and Tiger Moth, Fairey IIIB, IIIC, IIID, IIIF, Flycatcher, Ferret, Swordfish, Fulmar, Albacore, Firefly and Barracuda, Gloster Sea Gladiator, Gloucester Sparrowhawk, Grumman Martlet and Wildcat, Handley-Page Hendon, Hanley and Queen Bee, Hawker Hedgehog and Sea Hurricane, Nieuport Nightjar, Parnall Panther, Puffin and Plover, RAE 1921 Target, Sopwith Pup, 1½ Strutter, 2F.1 Camel and Snipe, Supermarine Seagull, Walrus and Seafire, Vickers Viking and Westland Walrus.

British balloon ships

Nearly every major, and some minor, navies experimented with manned captive balloons lofted from warships during the period 1862–1914 but there was no operational use of them after the American Civil War save briefly during the Russo-Japanese and Italo-Turkish wars. During World War I, however, balloons were used in hundreds of vessels, ranging from trawlers to battleships, in the navies of Great Britain, France, Italy and the United States.

These were kite balloons, which had been developed in the late nineteenth century, and which with a system of stabilizing vents and fins offered far steadier

Manica, the first British balloon ship, with kite balloon inflated in her forward well and wind screens raised. *Author's collection*

observation platforms than the classic spherical type that had existed since 1783.

The Russian navy, as noted elsewhere, had been the first to create a sea-going balloon ship, but it was quickly relegated to obscurity, and the Royal Navy was the only one during World War I to operate vessels especially equipped to handle balloons as a sole function. All were otherwise unnoteworthy mercantile conversions, outfitted basically the same way, with equipment for generation, compression and storage of hydrogen, apparatus for balloon inflation, winches to control a balloon's ascent and haul it down, rigging systems for towing the aerial craft clear of the ship, and usually some form of shelter for when it was on deck or in a hold. Hydrogen was the lifting element for all lighter-than-air craft during World War I, highly dangerous because of its extreme flammability. An American crash programme in 1917–18 developed mass production of nonflammable helium, until then extremely rare and costly, but its first product was still awaiting shipment when the war ended.

These balloon ships were employed primarily to assist naval operations against land but their work became less useful as the war continued, and they were phased out during 1916–17; three reverted to mercantile service, one was converted to a seaplane carrier and only one retained, to act as a depot ship for balloons embarked on warships.

The shipboard balloon as a means of aerial reconnaissance lingered on into the 1920s in the American, French, Japanese and Spanish navies but by the early '30s had disappeared, replaced by the aeroplane.

Interior of a balloon well, probably on *Manica*, with wind screens lowered. *Courtesy of P H Liddle*

MANICA

Displacement:	4120t (4186 tonnes)
Dimensions:	361ft bp × 47ft × 26ft (max)
	(110m × 14.3m × 7.9m)
Machinery:	1 set triple expansion, 1 shaft; 12kts
Armament:	1–12pdr LA, 1–3pdr AA; 2–6pdr AA added in 1916
Balloon arrangements:	Silicol gas generator, compressor, winch, wooden balloon platform forward replaced by balloon well in 1916; 1 kite balloon; 1 seaplane added in 1916
Complement:	unknown but included 89 balloon personnel

Name	Builder	Laid down	Launched	Completed	Fate
MANICA	Sir James Laing & Sons, Sunderland	?	1900	12.1900	?

This cargo vessel was hired by the Admiralty on 11 March 1915 (purchased later in 1915) for conversion to a balloon ship in response to a request for a balloon or man-lifting kite to help spot gunfire for the fleet at the Dardanelles. She had reportedly been built for the British & Colonial Steam Navigation Company but apparently belonged to Ellerman & Bucknall Steamship Company at the time of hiring. The conversion

was done in great haste, apparently by H Grayson & Company, at Birkenhead.

Manica arrived at Mudros on 9 April 1915, and 10 days later lofted her balloon to spot gunfire for a shore bombardment by cruiser *Bacchante*. On 25 April she spotted for gunfire during the Gallipoli troop landings and continued in that role off the peninsula until mid-September, rendering what was said to be highly valuable service.

Returning to Britain, she was given an extensive refit at Birkenhead by Cammell, Laird & Company which included replacement of the balloon platform with a well measuring 92ft (30.2m) × 30ft (9.8m), addition of extra AA armament and facilities for operating a seaplane. Assigned to East Africa, she arrived at Zanzibar in April 1916 and served extensively in support of coastal operations until May 1917.

After she ceased balloon service, it was proposed to convert her to a seaplane carrier but nothing came of the suggestion. She was renamed *Huntball* at Bombay on 20 August 1917 and served as a collier under the red ensign until 28 June 1918.

MENELAUS

Displacement:	4672grt (4747 tonnes)
Dimensions:	392ft pp × 47ft × 26ft (maximum)
	(119.4m × 14.3m × 7.9m)
Machinery:	1 set triple expansion, 1 shaft; 12kts
Armament:	nil
Balloon arrangements:	silicol gas generator, compressor, winch, balloon hold forward; 1 kite balloon
Complement:	unknown

Name	Builder	Laid down	Launched	Completed	Fate
MENELAUS	Scotts Shipbuilding & Engineering Company, Greenock	?	?	1895	?

HECTOR

Displacement:	4660grt (4734.8 tonnes)

All other particulars as *Menelaus*

Name	Builder	Laid down	Launched	Completed	Fate
HECTOR	Workman, Clark & Company, Belfast	?	1895	1896	?

Hector, with escorting trawler and destroyer, preparing to loft her balloon off the Gallipoli peninsula in 1915. *Menelaus* was virtually identical in appearance. *Courtesy of P H Liddle*

Impressed by *Manica*'s work at Gallipoli, the Admiralty took over these nearly identical vessels from the Ocean Steamship Company for conversion to balloon ships – *Menelaus* on 5 May 1915, *Hector* on 12 May. They were outfitted at the same time, also by the Grayson firm, in the same manner as *Manica*.

Menelaus was assigned to the Dover Patrol in July 1915 and was active in operations off the Belgian coast during the rest of that year and early 1916, lofting the balloon to spot fire for monitors during coastal bombardments. On occasion, she transferred the balloon to the trawler *Peary*, whose shallower draught permitted a closer approach to shore.

Menelaus was relieved at Dover by *City of Oxford* on 15 March 1916 and assigned to the fleet at Scapa Flow. There was little for her to do there, and, as the result of a decision by the Grand Fleet Aircraft Committee to phase out the balloon ships, she ceased lighter-than-air service on 7 June 1917 and subsequently became an ammunition carrier under the red ensign.

Hector was sent to supplement *Manica* in Gallipoli waters, arriving in the Aegean on 9 June 1915. With the evacuation of the peninsula in January 1916 she was withdrawn to Mudros. In March 1916 she was based at Mitylene Island to spot gunfire for warships against the Turkish coast as part of a feigned landing in the Gulf of Smyrna. Returning to Britain after this operation, she ceased balloon service in April, reverting to mercantile duty as an ammunition carrier, collier and troop ship until December 1918.

CITY OF OXFORD

Displacement:	7450t (7569.7 tonnes)
Dimensions:	421ft oa × 43ft × 26ft 6in (mean)
	(125.6m × 13.1m × 7.9m)
Machinery:	1 set vertical triple expansion, 1 shaft, 2500ihp = 10.5–12kts. 8925 nm at 10kts
Armament:	1–3in (76.2mm) LA, 2–6pdr AA
Balloon arrangements:	silicol gas generator, compressor, steam winch, wooden balloon platform forward; 1 kite balloon replaced by seaplanes in 1917
Complement:	unknown

Name	Builder	Laid down	Launched	Completed	Fate
CITY OF OXFORD	Barclay, Curle & Company, Belfast	?	6.1882	1882	?

City of Oxford as a balloon ship in 1916 or 1917. *Imperial War Museum*

City of Oxford after conversion to a seaplane
carrier with canvas aircraft shelters and handling
booms added. *Imperial War Museum*

City of Oxford was purchased by the Admiralty from
Ellerman & Bucknall Steamship Company on 28
October 1914 and rigged to resemble the dreadnaught
St Vincent as a unit of the Special Service Squadron
of dummy battleships, based at Scapa Flow from
December 1914 until mid-1915. She was virtually
rebuilt as a balloon ship by Harland & Wolff Ltd at
Belfast in work stretching from July 1915 to 9 March
1916. So extensive and efficient were the balloon
arrangements that she was officially described as 'the
ship which most nearly approached the ideal for
balloon service'.

City of Oxford relieved *Menelaus* at Dover on 15
March 1916 and took part in operations off the
Belgian coast until 4 August 1916 and then served
with the Battle Fleet at Scapa Flow from 9 August to
18 October 1916. On 22 October she joined the Battle
Cruiser Force at Rosyth as a balloon depot ship, active

Canning, last of the British balloon ships, with
her kite balloon ascending from the forward well.
Author's collection

in installation and maintenance of balloons on battle cruisers, light cruisers and destroyers.

With the decision to deactivate the balloon ships, she was converted for seaplane carrier duties at Hull from 1 April to late June 1917 but was given only canvas aircraft shelters instead of a permanent hangar.

She replaced *Anne* in the Egypt and East Indies Seaplane Squadron, arriving at Port Said on 8 August 1917 and was very active in operations off the Levan-

tine and Red Sea coasts until April 1918. Thereafter, she became a depot ship for Egypt Group seaplanes; she was based at Alexandria and Suez and fitted to accommodate six Short Type 184s and an unknown number of Sopwith Babys. She returned to home waters in late October 1918, and was paid off on 20 November. She was sold out of service in 1920, and returned to mercantile status.

CANNING

Displacement:	5366t (5452.2 tonnes)
Dimensions:	424ft pp × 52ft × 29ft
	(129.5m × 15.9m × 8.8m)
Machinery:	2 sets triple expansion, 3 double boilers, 2 shafts; 13kts
Armament:	1–6pdr LA, 2–6pdr AA
Balloon	
arrangements:	balloon well forward, electrolytic and silicol gas generators, compressor, steam winch, 600 hydrogen storage bottles; 1 kite balloon
Complement:	unknown

Name	Builder	Laid down	Launched	Completed	Fate
CANNING	D & W Henderson & Company, Glasgow	?	1896	6.1896	?

Largest of the balloon ships, *Canning* was hired by the Admiralty on 9 May 1915 (purchased on 28 June) from the Liverpool, Brazil & River Plate Steam Navigation Company. She was originally intended for use as a transport but instead was converted to a balloon ship by the Grayson firm at Birkenhead during June–September 1915.

She replaced *Manica* at Mudros on 7 October 1915 but took part in only a few minor operations before assisting in the Gallipoli evacuation during 10–17 December. She was next stationed at Salonika to assist in coastal operations. On 24 May 1916, she landed her balloon section for service ashore with the British army's 22nd Division and on 1 June sailed for

England carrying the wreckage of the German army Zeppelin LZ.85, which had been shot down at Salonika in May by British warships.

She was refitted at Birkenhead from 22 June to 4 December as a balloon depot ship, with the hydrogen storage capacity greatly increased. Arriving at Scapa Flow on 28 December 1916, *Canning* served with the Grand Fleet until January 1919, inflating and maintaining balloons for warships, so efficiently and speedily that she was retained in service well after the other balloon vessels had been paid off. She was sold to A D Axarlis of Greece on 21 January 1920, ending the history of the balloon ship in the Royal Navy.

Other balloon craft

In May 1915 the tug *Rescue* (357grt, completed in 1904, no other particulars known), which had been hired by the Admiralty on 23 March 1915 for use as a salvage vessel, was equipped with a spherical balloon for service off Gallipoli. The balloon was of Boer War vintage, part of the lighter-than-air *matériel* transferred from the British army to the Royal Navy during November 1913–January 1914. Apparently it was to be lofted as a decoy to draw fire away from the kite balloons, although manned ascents may have been contemplated or attempted. The project was abandoned after what was called 'a few days of unrewarded experiment'.

Shortly thereafter, because of the vulnerability of *Manica* to enemy artillery ashore, her hydrogen generator and compressor were transferred to *Rescue*, which was stationed at Imbros and would steam out to

inflate *Manica*'s balloon at sea. This arrangement ended when *Rescue* was assigned to assist in the Suvla Bay landing in August, and *Manica* re-embarked the gas apparatus.

Rescue remained in naval service until 14 June 1919, but her ultimate fate is unrecorded.

To supplement the balloon ships of the Dover Patrol, the Admiralty hired a steel barge named *Arctic* in January 1916. This craft, measuring 145ft (47.7m) × 26ft (8.5m), was converted by C & H Crichton at Liverpool. A hold was created to accommodate a balloon 82ft (26.9m) long and 22ft 6in (7.4m) in diameter and a dynamo installed to power an electric balloon winch.

Arctic was purchased upon completion of conversion in May 1916 and was towed to Dover with a temporary wooden deck over the balloon hold. It

took part in coastal operations, usually towed by a monitor, until November 1917, when it was detached to be 'utilized for other services', as an official description puts it. The barge was sold out of service on 14 January 1920.

Rescue carrying the vintage spherical balloon she operated briefly and unsuccessfully off Gallipoli in 1915. *Author's collection*

Catapult trials ship

SLINGER

Displacement:	875t (889 tonnes)
Dimensions:	unknown
Machinery:	steam engine, 1030ihp = 10kts
Armament:	nil
Aircraft arrangements:	catapult, 2 derricks
Complement:	unknown

Name	Builder	Laid down	Launched	Completed	Fate
SLINGER	Lobnitz & Company, Renfrew	?	?	9.1917	?

The Royal Navy had briefly considered the catapult before World War I but did not evince any real interest until 1916, when the Admiralty invited bids for hydraulic, electric and compressed air types. The hydraulic and electric types were not pursued but two compressed air types were produced. For shipboard tests of the model offered by Armstrong, Whitworth & Co, a steam hopper under construction was acquired and appropriately named *Slinger*.

The catapult, installed over the forecastle, could propel a weight of 5000lb (2272kg) at a maximum speed of 52.17kts but apparently was never tested at full power. In the first test, on 1 October 1917 while *Slinger* was tied up to a jetty on the Tyne, an unmanned Short 184 was launched, its fuselage fabric removed and its engine replaced by ballast. Ballasted Short floats were launched in later tests before the

vessel was transferred to the Experimental Aircraft Depot at the Isle of Grain, where trials continued under the direction of Lieutenant Colonel Harry R Busteed, RAF. The aircraft used was a Fairey F.127, a specially designed floatplane, stressed for catapult launching, of which only one example was produced.

Several successful launches were made, some while *Slinger* was under way, and the catapult seemed a practical proposition. Further development was not undertaken, however, because a catapult was deemed too cumbersome and space-consuming for shipboard installation, while at the same time it had been demonstrated that aircraft could be flown from shipboard platforms without need of a launching device.

Slinger was sold out of service on 16 October 1919, and no catapult was seen on a British warship until one was installed on *Vindictive* (qv) in 1925.

Catapult trials ship *Slinger* in 1917, probably at the Isle of Grain. *Imperial War Museum*

The Fairey F.127, a one-of-a-kind aircraft, on *Slinger*'s catapult during trials at the Isle of Grain in 1917. *J M Bruce/G S Leslie collection*

Aircraft-equipped submarine

In another of the many schemes for intercepting German airships over the North Sea, submarine *E22* was equipped at Harwich in early 1916 to carry two Sopwith Schneider floatplanes on parallel sloping rails that extended from aft of the conning tower to the aft deck casing. They were to be launched by trimming the boat down until they floated free for takeoff.

The first attempt, in early April, failed when the notoriously weak floats of the Sopwiths broke up in a choppy sea before they could take off. A second attempt may have been made with the same result. In a final try, the seaplanes were able to get aloft, and they flew back to their base at Felixstowe.

The idea was given up as impractical but the rails were not removed from *E22* before she was sunk on 25 April, taking with her the log that would have shed more light on this ill-documented experiment.

E22 rigged for surface running with two Sopwith Schneiders embarked during experiments in early 1916, probably at Harwich. The foremost Schneider is an early model with wing warping and a triangular fin and is unarmed; the second is a later standard version with aileron control, an enlarged fin and armed with a machine gun. *J M Bruce/G S Leslie collection*

E22 trimmed down aft with one Schneider afloat. *J M Bruce/G S Leslie collection*

E22 submerged even more aft, preparing to slide the second Schneider into the water. *J M Bruce/G S Leslie collection*

Caspian Sea seaplane carriers

Among the Russian merchant vessels taken over by the Royal Navy force operating against the Bolsheviks in the Caspian Sea in 1918–19 were *Orlionoch* (1406grt, completed in 1888) and *Alader Yousanoff* (2071grt, completed in 1905). Both were crudely equipped to carry two aircraft each, Short floatplanes from the RAF Caspian contingent commanded by Lieutenant Colonel (later Air Chief Marshal Sir) Frederick W Bowhill, who had been captain of *Empress* during the Cuxhaven Raid in 1914. *Orlionoch* was armed with two 4in guns and *Alader Yousanoff* with a single 12pdr.

Both operated aircraft in reconnaissance and bombing missions, *Orlionoch* from late 1918 and *Alader Yousanoff* from January 1919. At least one aircraft was lost in an accidental crash. *Alader Yousanoff* developed boiler defects in July 1919 and apparently was inactive after that. Both were turned over to the so-called White Russians in August 1919, upon the withdrawal of the British forces, and later fell into Bolshevik hands, eventually returning to mercantile service.

No other details are known about these ships and their fates are unrecorded, save that *Alader Yousanoff* may still have been afloat in World War II.

Russian steamer *Orlionoch* in British service as a seaplane carrier in the Caspian Sea, with two Short floatplanes embarked. *Author's collection*

Italy

The Italian navy's initial venture into aeronautics came in 1907, when the cruiser *Elba* was equipped with a kite balloon for manoeuvres off Sicily. Four years later, during the Italian conquest of Tripolitania, Italy fielded the world's first truly organized air force, a mixed bag of aircraft, airships and balloons responsible for a number of 'famous firsts' in the history of aerial warfare.

Cavalmarino with the kite balloon used briefly to direct fire of warships off the North African coast in 1911. *Author's collection*

Among them was the first Italian use of a craft that might be termed an aviation vessel, a brigantine named *Cavalmarino* that was stripped of her second mast and its rigging to provide space for a kite balloon. Towed by the naval tug *Ercole*, she lofted the balloon to spot gunfire for the cruiser *Carlo Alberto* and battleship *Re Umberto* against Turkish shore positions. This use ended abruptly on 12 December 1911 when the balloon was swept from *Cavalmarino*'s deck in a storm and was found ashore two days later, totally wrecked.

An Italian naval air arm, the *Sezione Avizione Marina*, was formally established in 1913, but grew slowly. It was equipped entirely with foreign aircraft. No attention was paid to shipboard aviation save for the brief experimental embarcation of a seaplane on the battleship *Dante Alighieri* and perhaps on the cruiser *San Marco* in 1913.

When Italy entered World War I in May 1915 the naval air arm consisted of about thirty aircraft, including three seaplanes tended by the cruiser *Elba* – all foreign makes. The first indigenous Italian seaplane was the Macchi L.1, produced by the aircraft division of the coach-building firm of Società Anonima Nieuport-Macchi at Varese; it was an almost exact copy of an Austro-Hungarian Lohner flying boat captured intact on 27 May 1915.

The Macchi designers caught up quickly, however, and the firm began turning out a variety of seaplanes, including nimble flying boat fighters, which equipped the Italian navy during, and for a long time after, World War I. Macchis and various models of FBA flying boats, many built under licence, were the dominant Italian naval aircraft during 1915–18 and the only types to see shipboard use (aside from four French

Nieuport VI floatplanes that *Elba* added to her brood at Brindisi between September 1915 and January 1916).

Italy, like Austria-Hungary, had little need for aviation vessels in the narrow confines of the Adriatic. That accounts for the fact that apart from *Elba* and *Europa* (qv), the only other aviation ships were two powered balloon lighters, *Luigi Mina* and *Umberto Missana*, of 205 and 290 metric tons, respectively, built at the La Spezia Royal Navy Yard in 1916 and 1917, propelled by petrol engines and each equipped with a kite balloon and 4-3in/30 (76.2mm) AA guns.

Europa at Valona in 1918 with hangars fully open. The aircraft suspended from her derricks are five **FBA Type H** reconnaissance planes and a Macchi M.5 fighter, all flying boats. *US Naval Historical Center via Christopher C Wright*

EUROPA

Displacement:	6275t (6400 tonnes) normal, 8664t (8805 tonnes) full load, 4134grt
Dimensions:	405ft 2in × 46ft 3in × 19ft 2in normal (123.18m × 14.07m × 5.86m) 25ft full load (7.62m)
Machinery:	1 set triple expansion, 1 shaft, 3000ihp = 12.2 kts, 2750 nm at 11.5kts
Armament:	2–3in/30 (76.2mm) AA
Aircraft arrangements:	large fixed hangars fore and aft, dimensions unknown; 8 aircraft
Complement:	?

Name	Builder	Laid down	Launched	Completed	Fate
EUROPA, ex-QUARTO, ex-SALACIA, ex-MANILA	Charles Connell & Company, Scotstoun, Glasgow	?	4.8.1895	?	BU, 1920 or 1921

This British merchant vessel's name was originally *Manila*, changed to *Salacia* when purchased by the Donaldson Line in 1898 and retained after coming under German ownership in 1911. It was changed to *Quarto* when purchased by the Italian Tito Campanella & Company in 1913 and changed to *Europa* after purchase from that firm by the Italian navy on 6 February 1915 for conversion to a depot ship for seaplanes and submarines.

The conversion was done at the La Spezia Royal Navy Yard from 20 February to May 1915 but the vessel was not formally commissioned until 6 October 1915. She was stationed at Brindisi from 13 October 1915 to 28 January 1916 and then at the Albanian port of Valona (now Vlore) until 13 November 1918. She was stricken for scrapping on 10 October 1920.

Europa served purely as a harbour-based tender. Her aerial complement varied from time to time, being originally six fighter and two reconnaissance planes. In early 1918 it was designated *258a Squadriglia Ricognizione* and consisted of two Macchi M.5 flying boat fighters and six FBA Type H reconnaissance flying boats.

Europa, probably at Valona, with her hangars partly open. Her hangars, like those of the German carriers, opened to the side. *Courtesy of Jacques Szynka*

Japan

The Japanese navy's initial association with aeronautics can be traced to 1876–77 with construction of hot-air and coal-gas balloons at the Naval Academy. Two Japanese-designed kite balloons were employed by the Japanese army at the siege of Port Arthur in 1904–5 and in August 1904 a naval observer suspended from one of them spotted fire for a naval shore battery against Russian ships in the harbour. Two battleships were damaged in this first use of an aerial device to direct gunfire against a purely naval target.

The first Japanese ventures into heavier-than-air flight began in 1909 under the aegis of a joint committee from three government ministries. Japanese naval interest was stirred during the next three years by demonstration flights performed by visiting foreign aviators, and in June 1912 an aeronautical department was established under the navy's Technical Bureau, construction of a naval air station on Tokyo Bay was authorized and six junior officers dispatched for flight training in the United States and Europe. Two of them returned later that year with the navy's first seaplanes – two Maurice Farman twin-float models from France and two single-float Curtiss types from the United States.

There was an immediate preference for the Farman, and manufacture of a modified version of it was undertaken at the Yokosuka Naval Arsenal. Three of this type plus a higher-powered model imported in 1914 equipped the seaplane carrier *Wakamiya Maru* at Tsingtao, as described below. This campaign not only marked the first employment of an aviation vessel in combat but produced what could be termed the first air-sea battle when on 27 November the Farmans tried unsuccessfully to bomb German and Austro-Hungarian warships in Kiaochow Bay.

Wakamiya Maru with a boom lowered to recover a Farman floatplane taxiing toward the ship. *Author's collection*

Wakamiya Maru rigged as a seaplane carrier with canvas hangars fore and aft. *Courtesy of K Stanley Yamashita*

With the fall of Tsingtao, Japanese naval aviation ceased combat in World War I. The only other Japanese vessel to embark aircraft during the remainder of the conflict was the auxiliary cruiser *Chikezen Maru*, which carried two floatplanes for a fruitless search for the German commerce raider *Wolf* in the Indian Ocean in October 1917.

More influential than the *Wakamiya Maru*'s operation were recommendations from Japanese observers with the Royal Navy, one of whom was aboard HMS *Furious* for a time, for a true aircraft-carrying vessel. These resulted ultimately in the authorization for the *Hosho*, the world's first designed-from-scratch, built-from-the-keel, flight-deck carrier to hit the water. Her construction was an example of faith in the future, as *Hosho* was projected before there were any aircaft suitable for her. The Sopwith Pup, used in the takeoff experiments that were preliminary to those expected on *Hosho*, was one of a large number of Pups purchased immediately after the war, and was hopelessly obsolete by 1920.

This situation began to be remedied in 1921 with the arrival of a British aviation mission composed of RAF and RNAS veterans headed by Colonel the Master of Sempill (William Francis Forbes-Sempill, later Lord Sempill). This group tutored the Japanese in all aspects of naval flying and laid the real foundations of Japanese naval air power. A concomitant was the purchase of a large number of British aircraft of several types, and the issue of licences for Japanese manufacture of British models. At the same time, the Mitsubishi industrial combine hired for its aeronautical divisions a British design team from the recently collapsed Sopwith Aviation Company, headed by the extremely talented Herbert Smith, who had designed many of the most famous Sopwith aircraft of World War I. This group quickly produced four basic carrier-type aircraft: a fighter, a reconnaissance-bomber and two torpedo planes. Thus, British aircraft, imported, licence-built or built from British designs, dominated Japanese flight decks, launching platforms and finally catapults until the early 1930s, when a program of replacement with all-Japanese designs was undertaken.

Meanwhile, the success of *Hosho* had helped influence the decision to convert two incomplete capital ships into carriers, as allowed under the Washington Treaty. They were the famous *Kaga* and *Akagi*.

WAKAMIYA MARU/WAKAMIYA

Displacement:	7720t (7844 tonnes), 4421grt
Dimensions:	365ft pp × 48ft 2in × 19ft
	(111.2m × 14.6m × 5.8m)
Machinery:	1 set vertical triple expansion, 3 boilers, 1 shaft, 1600shp = 9.5kts. Coal: 851t (987 tonnes)
Armament:	(1914) 2–3in/40 (76.2mm) LA; 2–47mm LA added later
Aircraft arrangements:	canvas hangars fore and aft; 4 aircraft
Complement:	?

Name	Builder	Laid down	Launched	Completed	Fate
WAKAMIYA, ex-WAKAMIYA MARU, ex-LETHINGTON	R Duncan & Co, Port Glasgow	?	21.9.1901	?	BU? 1931?

The W R Rea Shipping Company's freighter *Lethington* was seized off Okinawa on 12 January 1905 by the Japanese torpedo boat *No 72* while bound for a Russian port during the Russo-Japanese War and adjudicated a legal prize. She was taken into Japanese service as a transport on 1 September 1905 under the name *Wakamiya Maru* and in 1908 was leased to the NYK line. She re-entered naval service as an auxiliary in late 1913 and operated one or two Farman floatplanes during October and November of that year in the first use of aircraft in Japanese naval manoeuvres.

She apparently was inactive for a time after that, but on 17 August 1914 was re-commissioned as a seaplane carrier, with canvas hangars added fore and aft.

On 1 September 1914, she joined the Second Squadron for operations against the German city/fortress/port of Tsingtao on the Chinese mainland, operating four Farman floatplanes, the first flight being made on 5 September. Damaged by striking a mine on 30 September, she was shored up temporarily for return to Sasebo for permanent repair, leaving her aircraft to operate from a beach base. She returned them to Japan in December after the conclusion of the Tsingtao campaign.

The vessel was rerated as an aircraft depot ship on 1 June 1915, with the mercantile suffix dropped from the name, and assigned to the Yokosuka naval air station. She was reclassified as an aircraft carrier on 1 April 1920 and in June of that year was fitted with a 66½ft (20m) platform over her forecastle from which Lieutenant (later Vice Admiral) Torao Kuwabara made the first Japanese shipboard takeoffs in a British Sopwith Pup. *Wakamiya* was inactive after 1 December 1925 and was stricken from the navy list on 1 April 1931, presumably for breaking up.

Wakamiya in the early 1920s; although rated, at the time, as an aircraft carrier with the mercantile suffix dropped from the name, she no longer carried the canvas hangars. *Author's collection*

Hosho during sea trials, with the original island configuration. *Courtesy of K Stanley Yamashita*

HOSHO

Displacement:	7470t (7590 tonnes) standard
Dimensions:	552ft ao × 59ft 1in × 20ft 3in (mean)
	(168.3m × 18m × 6.1m)
Machinery:	2 sets geared turbines, 8 boilers, 2 shafts, 30,000shp (31,117shp on trials) = 25kts (26.6kts on trials); 8690 nm at 12kts, 2170 nm at 25kts. Oil: 2695t (3128 tonnes). Coal: 940t (955 tonnes)
Armament:	4–5.5in/50 (140mm) LA 4 × 1, 2–3in/40 (76.2m) AA 2 × 1; 3in replaced by 12–13.2mm AA (3 × 4) in 1936, 8–25mm AA (4 × 2) added in 1941; 5.5in replaced by 8–25mm AA (4 × 2) in 1942; armament reduced to 6–25mm AA in 1945
Aircraft arrangements:	flight deck 519ft 4in (170.8m) extended in 1944 to 593ft 3in (180.8m) × 74ft 6in (26m) maximum; forward lift 42ft (12.8m) × 27ft 11in (8.5m), aft lift 44ft 11in (13.7m) × 23ft (7m) 15 aircraft normal, 26 maximum reduced to 21 in 1934
Complement:	550

Name	Builder	Laid down	Launched	Completed	Fate
HOSHO, ex-HIRYU	Asano Shipbuilding Co, Tsurumi	16.12.1919	13.11.1921	7.12.1922	BU, 1947

This vessel was authorized on 12 March 1918 under the 8-6 Fleet Project as one of six auxiliaries rated as transports, five of which were completed as tankers. For this reason it has sometimes been incorrectly stated that *Hosho* was redesigned from tanker configuration. In fact, she was designed and built from the keel as a flight-deck carrier – the first in the world, completed fourteen months before the British *Hermes* although that vessel had been laid down and launched earlier. She was originally named *Hiryu*, changed in 1920 to *Hosho* (Flying Phoenix). Another carrier, similar to *Hosho* but 3000 tons heavier, to have been named *Shokaku*, was authorized in 1922 but was cancelled under the terms of the Washington Treaty before having been laid down.

Hosho was completed with a small starboard island, tripod mast and three funnels hinged for lowering when aircraft were landing or taking off. The island and mast were removed in 1923, ostensibly because they interfered with aircraft landing but actually to correct instability caused by inadequate metacentric height. The original arresting-gear system consisted of fore-and-aft lines in the British pattern but was later changed to a lateral-line system. In 1934 the

Vickers Viking amphibian flown by Lieutenant Commander Herbert G Brackley of the British Aviation Mission to Japan landing aboard *Hosho*, March 1923. The funnels have been lowered and the flight deck has the original fore-and-aft arresting gear system. *Author's collection*

Hosho running at speed, with one aircraft far forward on the flight deck. *Courtesy of K Stanley Yamashita*

hinged funnels were fixed in permanent vertical position, and maximum aircraft capacity reduced to twenty-one. Modifications just before and during the Pacific war included extension of the flight deck, refixture of the funnels, this time in permanent horizontal position, and replacement of the LA battery with increasing numbers of light AA guns.

The first landing on *Hosho* was made on 23 February 1923 by William L Jordan, a test pilot for Mitsubishi International Combustion Engine Com-

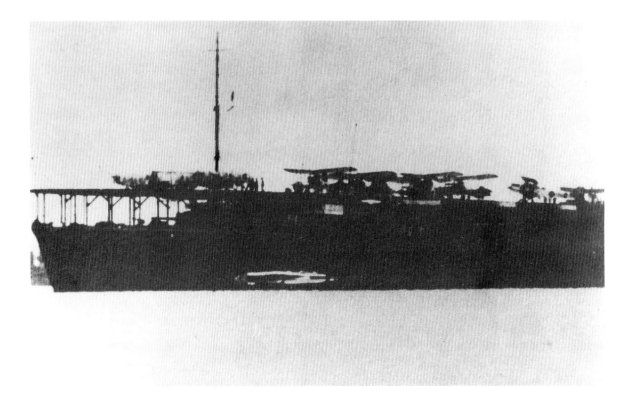

pany, in a British-designed Mitsubishi Type 10 (1MF5) fighter; the first landing by a Japanese pilot on 16 March 1923 by Lieutenant (later Rear Admiral) Shunichi Kira, also in a Mitsubishi Type 10.

Hosho took part in operations off the China coast in 1939–40 during the Sino-Japanese conflict, but by late 1941 was judged too small and slow for work with the fleet and was relegated to secondary and training duties. She did accompany the Japanese main body during the Midway operation but, after that, was used solely for pilot training.

She was damaged by US air attack on 19 March 1945 at Kure and was surrendered there in August 1945. Postwar she was used to repatriate Japanese troops from the Asian mainland, with a portion of the forward flight deck removed, until 16 August 1946. She was broken up at Osaka in 1947.

During her long career, *Hosho* operated nearly every type of Japanese shipboard aircraft, from the Mitsubishi Type 10 fighters and reconnaissance-bombers of the early 1920s to the torpedo planes of the 1940s. For the Midway operation, she reportedly carried eight obsolescent Aichi D1A2 dive bombers (Allied code name Susie); if so, this would surely be the last time a Japanese carrier operated biplanes. She was obsolescent by World War II but had proved invaluable in pioneering techniques of carrier operation and in training junior air officers who would rise to high rank.

An otherwise undistinguished view of *Hosho* during the early 1930s shows the island superstructure and tripod mast replaced with a simple pole mast. Identifiable aircraft on deck are Nakajima A1N1-2 fighters, a licence-built version of the British Gloster Gambet, and Mitsubishi B2M1-2 torpedo-bombers, a British Blackburn design. *Courtesy of K Stanley Yamashita*

Russia

Russian transport *Kolyma* preparing to loft a locally built spherical balloon at Vladivostok, late 1904. Forward of the balloon a large canvas windscreen has been erected. *S F Post photo, author's collection*

The Imperial Russian Navy became interested in aeronautics shortly after the adoption of the balloon for army service in 1884 and by the mid-1890s had established 'aerostatic parks' on the Baltic and Black Sea coasts. By the time of the Russo-Japanese War, a good many experiments with towing balloons and man-lifting kites from warships had been conducted.

Further experimentation with shipboard balloons was carried out in 1904–5 during the war at Vladivostok, by an army engineer captain, Fyodor A Postnikov,

Kolyma at Vladivostok in 1905 with a kite balloon that has been shortened to permit its deck carriage.
S F Post photo, author's collection

Armoured cruiser *Rossia* at Vladivostok in 1905 with the kite balloon she employed both experimentally and operationally. *S F Post photo, author's collection*

A closer view of the kite balloon riding over *Rossia*'s quarterdeck just before the start of the raiding cruise of May 1905. Armoured cruiser *Gromoboi*, which accompanied *Rossia*, is in the background. *S F Post photo, author's collection*

Facing page: The Black Sea Fleet's carrier division, early 1917. The vessels are, from left, *Imperator Nikolai I*, *Imperator Alexandr I* and *Rumania*. The fourth ship may be *Almaz*. This division and the British East Indies and Egypt Seaplane Squadron were the only formally organized carrier units of World War I. *Boris V Drashpil collection*

who had been trained in aeronautics at St Petersburg. (Postnikov emigrated to the United States after the war, anglicized his name to Post, and continued work in aeronautics. He has often, therefore, been confused with the well-known American balloonist of the period, Augustus Post.) Using spherical types manufactured locally and at least one kite balloon dispatched overland, Postnikov and his crews made frequent ascents from a variety of vessels, including the transports *Argun*, *Kamchadal* and *Kolyma*. The latter was modified for balloon use by removal of the mainmast and installation of canvas wind shields.

A balloon was also operated from the armoured cruiser *Rossia*, flagship of the Vladivostok cruiser squadron, in experiments with mine detection, trials of various forms of air-to-sea communications and direction of gunfire during practice against shore targets.

From 9 to 11 May 1904, *Rossia*, accompanied by the armoured cruiser *Gromoboi*, carried a balloon on a raiding cruise into the Sea of Japan; this was the first attempt by a warship to employ a balloon in a wartime high-seas operation. Thirteen successful ascents were made from the cruiser's deck until mooring lines were broken while the balloon was aloft but unmanned. It came down on the sea, was towed back to the vessel and manhandled aboard, too damaged for further use. Postnikov later claimed that several Japanese ships were captured after having been spotted from the balloon, but this is belied by his own log of the operation, and there is complete lack of confirmation in any other source.

The Vladivostok balloon activity, virtually unknown even to Russian aero historians for decades, was imaginative and highly interesting, but contributed nothing to the conduct of the war because of the isolation of that port from the conflict; neither did another interesting venture under way at the same time in the Baltic.

What might very well be called a Russian carrier-battleship task force at Sevastopol, about 1916. The vessels are, from left, carrier *Imperator Nikolai I* or *Imperator Alexandr I*, battleship *Rostislav*, battleship *Tri Sviatitelia*, unidentified ship, carrier *Imperator Nikolai I* or *Imperator Alexandr I* and battleship *Pantelimon*. *Boris V Drashpil collection*

RUSS

Displacement:	9600t (9754 tonnes), 5681grt
Dimensions:	449ft × 49ft × 22ft
	(136.6m × 14.9m × 6.7m)
Machinery:	triple expansion, 1 shaft, 9500ihp = 17–19kts
Armament:	?
Aircraft arrangements:	clear deck aft for balloon inflation and handling, 3 electrolytic hydrogen generators, hydrogen compression equipment, winches; 9 balloons
Complement:	total unknown but included 118 aeronautical personnel

Name	Builder	Laid down	Launched	Completed	Fate
RUSS, ex-LAHN	Fairfield Shipbuilding & Engineering Co, Govan, Glasgow	?	1887	?	?

A passenger vessel built for the North German Lloyd Line's Atlantic service under the name *Lahn*, this ship was purchased after the outbreak of the Russo-Japanese War with funds donated by a wealthy former Russian naval officer. Her conversion to a balloon ship was taken in hand at Libau in November 1904 under supervision of Lieutenant M N Bolshev, a pioneer in Russian naval use of balloons and man-lifting kites.

The conversion was thorough and ingenious, making *Russ* the world's first true aviation ship, in the sense of an oceangoing, self-propelled vessel intended specifically for aeronautical service, and also the first to carry a multiple number of aerial devices. The mainmast and a portion of the aft superstructure were removed to provide a clear upper-deck space for balloon inflation and handling. The hydrogen generators, compression equipment and containers occu-

pied three deck levels below, and were powered by an independent auxiliary system of steam engines and dynamos. For air-to-ship communication, 1000 metres of telephone line was stowed. Cameras and associated equipment were provided for aerial photography (which was pioneered by the Russian navy). The balloon component included four kite balloons, one spherical type for observation and four small kite balloons for signalling.

Unfortunately, this ingenuity was wasted, for *Russ* was decrepit, after years of hard service in the Atlantic, with rusty and much-patched boilers. Rated as a second-class cruiser, she was to have sailed with the Third Pacific Fleet in March 1905 but failed to do so because of general unseaworthiness. At least one source, however, states that she sailed independently later, and proceeded as far as Spain before being recalled. In either case it seems fortunate, for she could

An artist's depiction in 1905 of *Russ*, the first true aviation ship, showing what appears to be an inflated kite balloon on the quarterdeck. The picture indicates that the vessel was armed, but details of her armament cannot be traced. *Boris V Drashpil collection*

Almaz rigged as a seaplane carrier with handling boom on mainmast. *Soviet State Naval Museum via Edgar Meos*

hardly have survived Tsushima. (Some confusion in this regard has been created by the fact that another auxiliary named *Russ* was sunk at Tsushima.)

Russ was stricken 21 November 1906 and sold for mercantile service. Her aeronautical equipment was reportedly turned over to the Russian army. She was later listed as a naval auxiliary in the Baltic during World War I, but her fate is unknown.

The Russian navy entered heavier-than-air aviation

in March 1910, with the dispatch of three officers to flight schools in France; the first aircraft were ordered from France later that year. A flying school was opened near St Petersburg still later in 1910, but this activity was soon concentrated mainly at Sevastopol on the Black Sea, where a more favourable climate permitted training for more months of the year.

During 1912–14 the naval air arm was composed largely of Curtiss floatplanes and flying boats of which a large but unknown number were ordered. In late 1914, these began to be phased out in favour of the indigenously designed and manufactured Grigorovich M-series flying boats, which constituted the main strength of naval aviation through the war.

A few proposals for aviation vessels were advanced before the war, but the only known experiment in shipboard use of aircraft was in early 1913, when a Curtiss floatplane was briefly embarked on the Black Sea Fleet cruiser *Kagul*.

Shipboard aviation was a wartime innovation, inaugurated in early 1915 with the conversion to seaplane carriers of three vessels in the Black Sea and one in the Baltic. By early 1917, the Russian navy possessed the world's second most powerful seaplane carrier force, outmatched numerically only by the Royal Navy but rivalling it in aggression and efficiency.

In some operations against the Turkish and Bulgarian coasts, the Black Sea Fleet can be said to have created the first carrier-battleship task force, with the capital ships subordinated to the carriers as the main striking arm of the combination. These operations alone refute the standard myth of Western historians that the Russian navy of World War I was a trivial and inefficient coastal defence appendage of the army, lacking vigour, valour and influence.

Grigorovich M.9 serial number 57 being hoisted aboard *Almaz*, 17 March 1915, a view showing the profile of this mainstay of Russian shipboard aviation. *Boris V Drashpil collection*

ALMAZ

Displacement:	3285t (3337 tonnes)
Dimensions:	363ft oa × 43ft 6in × 17ft 6in
	(110.6m × 13.3m × 5.3m)
Machinery:	triple expansion, 2 shafts, 7500ihp = 19kts
Armament:	7–4.7in/? (120mm) 7 × 1, 4–3in/? (76.2mm) AA 4 × 1
Armour:	deck 3in (76.2mm)
Aircraft arrangements:	handling platforms for seaplanes hoisted by boom on mainmast; 3–4 aircraft
Complement:	340

Name	Builder	Laid down	Launched	Completed	Fate
ALMAZ	Baltic Works, St Petersburg	25.9.1902	2.6.1903	1904	BU 1934

A hybrid cruiser/yacht, rated as a third-class cruiser and intended to serve as a viceroyal yacht in the Far East, *Almaz* sailed with the Second Pacific Squadron in March 1904 and survived the Battle of Tsushima. She returned to the Baltic after the Russo-Japanese War but, before World War I, was assigned to the Black Sea Fleet as a dispatch vessel.

In early 1915 she was outfitted for use as a seaplane carrier, but when and where is not known. As the speediest of the Black Sea Fleet's carriers, she took part independently or in conjunction with other carriers in operations off the Bosporus and Turkish European coast from March to May 1915 and in raids on Varna, Bulgaria, in October 1915 and August 1916.

She served as a Bolshevik headquarters ship after the November Revolution but was later seized by

French interventionist forces at Odessa and turned over to White Russian authorities. In 1920, she sailed with other ex-czarist vessels to Algiers. All were taken over by France in 1928 and *Almaz* was scrapped in 1934.

Although this photo is of poor quality, necessitating retouching, it is of interest because it shows the seaplane handling platform abaft the mainmast on *Almaz*, 13 March 1916. The aircraft is a Grigorovich flying boat. *Boris V Drashpil collection*

ORLITZA

Displacement:	3800grt (3861 tonnes)
Dimensions:	300ft × 40ft × 18ft
	(91.5m × 12.2m × 5.2m)
Machinery:	vertical triple expansion, 2200ihp = 12kts
Armament:	8–3in/? (76.2mm) 8 × 1, 2 MG
Aircraft arrangements:	steel framework canvas-shielded hangars fore and aft, dimensions unknown, 4–9 aircraft
Complement:	?

Name	Builder	Laid down	Launched	Completed	Fate
ORLITZA, ex-IMPERATRIZA ALEXSANDRA, ex-WOLOGDA	Caldeon Ship-Building & Engineering Company, Dundee	?	?	1903	?

Russia's only Baltic aviation vessel in World War I, this cargo-passenger liner had been in mercantile service under two names before being acquired for conversion to a seaplane carrier, probably at St Petersburg, and commissioned as *Orlitza* on 2 February 1915.

She served mainly in the Gulf of Riga area during 1915–17, active in defence against German naval operations around Moon Sound, the Straits of Irben and Osel Island. Her aircraft, sometimes based on the coast or on inland lakes, were also active against the flank of the German army on the Courland coast.

Orlitza, the Russian navy's only Baltic Sea carrier, with covers furled on the aft hangar, down on the forward hangar. *Soviet State Naval Museum via Edgar Meos*

By April 1918 she was immobilized at Helsingfors (now Helsinki), Finland, with other units of the Baltic Fleet, but with a skeleton crew she sailed to Kronstadt that month in what has become celebrated in Soviet naval history as 'the voyage through the ice'. She appears to have been inactive during the rest of the Russian civil war, but some of her personnel helped organize Bolshevik naval aviation on the Volga.

Orlitza re-entered mercantile service, reportedly the first vessel to do so under the Soviet flag, in 1919, renamed *Soviet*. She is believed to have remained afloat until at least 1939 but her fate is unknown.

Orlitza in 1917. A Grigorovich flying boat is in the forward hangar, and this view shows the forward armament. *Soviet State Naval Museum via Edgar Meos*

Imperator Nikolai I, probably at Sevastopol. She is distinguished from her near sister, *Imperator Alexandr I*, by a dark band on the funnel. *Soviet State Naval Museum via Edgar Meos*

Imperator Alexandr I with Grigorovich flying boats carried aft. Like her near sister, *Imperator Nikolai I*, she has been fitted with aircraft handling booms on the mainmast. *Soviet State Naval Museum via Edgar Meos*

IMPERATOR NIKOLAI I

Displacement: 9230t (9378 tonnes)
Dimensions: 381ft oa × 52ft × 26ft mean (116m × 15.8m × 7.9m) 28ft full load (8.5m)
Machinery: triple expansion, 4 boilers, 2 shafts, 5100ihp = 13.5kts
Armament: 6–4.7in/? (120mm) 6 × 1, 4–3in/? (76.2mm) 4 × 1
Aircraft
arrangements: no hangars, aircraft handled on deck; 6–8 aircraft
Complement: ?

Name	Builder	Laid down	Launched	Completed	Fate
IMPERATOR NIKOLAI I	John Brown & Company, Clydebank	?	?	1913	Believed lost in World War II, cause uncertain

IMPERATOR ALEXANDR I

Displacement: 9240t (9388 tonnes)
Dimensions: as *Imperator Nikolai I* but with probably slightly deeper draught
Machinery: as *Imperator Nikolai I* but 15kts
Armament: as *Imperator Nikolai I*
Aircraft
arrangements: as *Imperator Nikolai I*
Complement: ?

Name	Builder	Laid down	Launched	Completed	Fate
IMPERATOR ALEXANDR I, ex-IMPERATOR ALEXANDR III	William Denny & Sons, Dumbarton	?	?	1914	Believed lost in World War II, cause uncertain

Grigorovich M.9 serial number 32 attached to a hoisting boom on *Imperator Nikolai I* or *Imperator Alexandr I*, 1915 or 1916. The aircraft is about to be lifted aboard. *Boris V̆ Drashpil collection*

These handsome cargo-liners, sisters save for slight disparity in tonnage and speed, were built for the Black Sea-Egyptian routes of the Russian Steam Navigation Trading Company and requisitioned as naval auxiliaries after the outbreak of war in 1914. They were converted into seaplane carriers in early 1915, though where and when is uncertain, with *Imperator Alexandr III* being renamed *Imperator Alexandr I* to avoid confusion with a battleship of the former name under construction at Nikolaev. Rated as *gidrokreisera* (hydro-cruisers) from the Russian designation for hydroaeroplanes (seaplanes), they formed a special division of the Black Sea Fleet. Modifications involved little beyond clearance of the aft upper deck for aircraft carriage and installation of handling booms on the mainmast, but they turned out to be extremely efficient carriers, especially proficient in rapid launching and recovery of seaplanes.

From March 1915, they were active in numerous operations against shipping and ports on the Turkish European and Anatolian coasts, and took part in raids on Varna in October 1915 and August 1916. On 6 February 1916, their aircraft sank the Turkish collier *Irmingard*, the largest (4211grt) merchant ship lost to air attack in World War I.

After the popular revolution of early 1917, they were renamed in response to the spirit of the new regime, *Nikolai* becoming *Respublikanetz* and *Alexandr* becoming *Aviator*. Inactive after April 1917, both vessels were taken over by France during the period of Allied intervention in the Russian civil war and eventually entered mercantile service with Cie Massageries Maritimes, renamed *Pierre Loti* and *Lamartine* respectively. Both were lost in World War II, but the circumstances are not known.

RUMINIA

Displacement:	3152grt (3202.6 tonnes)
Dimensions:	355ft 3in × 42ft × 15ft
	(108m × 12.6m × 4.6m)
Machinery:	vertical triple expansion, 5 boilers, 2 shafts, 7200ihp = 18.5kts
Armament:	4–6in/? (152mm) 4 × 1, 4–3in/? (76.2mm) AA 4 × 1
Aircraft arrangements:	decks cleared for aircraft carriage aft and amidships, handling booms on mainmast, 1–4 aircraft
Complement:	?

Name	Builder	Laid down	Launched	Completed	Fate
RUMINIA	? (French)	?	1904	?	?

This vessel, whose name can also be spelt *Roumania* or *Romania*, was built in France. She was one of five merchantmen of the Romanian State Maritime Service which served as aircraft-carrying auxiliaries with the

Ruminia, best-equipped of the aircraft-carrying Romanian merchantmen that joined the Black Sea Fleet in 1917. She is carrying Grigorovich flying boats aft and amidships. *Soviet State Naval Museum via Edgar Meos*

Black Sea Fleet after Romania became a co-belligerent in August 1916. She was the best equipped for aviation service, the only one rated as an aviation vessel – *gidroviotransport* (hydroplane transport) – and the only one to operate aircraft other than incidentally. She was renamed *Rouminskaya Respublika* in early 1917.

Names and what particulars are known of the others are:

Dakia and *Imperator Trayan* (sister ships), auxiliary cruisers: 3147grt, 4–5.9in (150mm) and possible 4– 3in (76.2mm) AA, 18kts, 3 aircraft; renamed *1907 God* (Year 1907) and *Sozialnaya Revolutzia* respectively in early 1917.

Principesa Maria, net layer: 1605grt, 18kts, 1 aircraft; probably renamed in early 1917.

Regele Carol I (also given as *Korol Carl*), minelayer: 2653grt, 306ft 7in (93.2m) × 42ft (12.8m) × 16 (5m), 2–5.9in (150mm), 28 mines, 1 aircraft; renamed *Ion Roate* in early 1917; completed in 1898, lost in 1941.

All these vessels were returned to Romania some time during 1917–19, and their fates are not known.

KOMMUNA

Displacement:	836.3 to 885.5t (850 to 900 tonnes)
Dimensions:	460ft × 63ft × 6ft
	(139.7m × 19m × 1.8m)
Speed under tow:	7.5 to 11kts

No details of construction or other particulars known

This large petroleum barge was equipped in August 1918 to carry aircraft for service with the Bolshevik Volga River flotilla. Usually towed by a sidewheel paddle tug, she carried up to nine Grigorovich M.9 flying boats and three Nieuport fighter aircraft. Lifts were fitted on each side to lower and recover the seaplanes. It is possible that the aeroplanes could take off from the long deck, but that is not confirmed.

Kommuna's aircraft were active in the civil war fighting along the Volga, their riverine mobility reportedly making them an important element of Bolshevik aerial strength, but details about the career of this highly unusual and ingenious craft are not known.

An approximate representation of the Volga River aircraft barge *Kommuna. Drawing by Kenn Davis from material provided by Jacek G Kolodziejczyk*

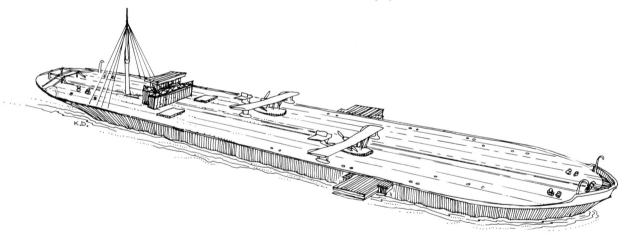

Spain

The Spanish navy's only aviation vessel, until after World War II, was unique in being equipped to operate airships as well as seaplanes and balloons. It was also distinctive as the only European aviation vessel to see combat between the end of the Russian civil war and the start of World War II.

Dédalo kicking up water as she goes astern with a deckload of Savoia flying boats. *Spanish Navy via Michael Burgess*

DÉDALO

Displacement:	10,800t (10,973 tonnes) standard
Dimensions:	420ft × 55ft × 29ft (maximum)
	(127m × 16.7m × 9.5m)
Machinery:	1 set quadruple expansion, 3 boilers, 1 shaft, 3140ihp = 10kts, 3000 nm at 10kts. Coal: 900t (940 tonnes)
Armament:	2–4.1in/40 or 45 (105mm) AA (?) 2 × 1, 2–57mm LA 2 × 1
Aircraft arrangements:	seaplane deck 197ft (60m) × 56ft (17m), 2 handling booms, 1 lift, balloon and airship well, aircraft mooring mast, hydrogen generation and compression equipment; 25 aircraft (maximum), 2 kite balloons
Complement:	324–398

Name	Builder	Laid down	Launched	Completed	Fate
DÉDALO, ex-NEUENFELS	Wigham Richardson & Company, Newcastle	?	?	5.1901	Sank while being broken up, 1940

The figures are derived from Spanish sources; those from English-language sources give a lighter draught and 12.5kts instead of 10kts.

The 5650grt *Neuenfels* of the Deutsche Dampfschiffahrts-Gesellschaft 'Hansa' line was one of six German freighters interned in Spain during World War I and awarded to that nation after the armistice, as partial reparation for mercantile losses inflicted by U-boats. They were designated *España* Nos 1 to 6; No 6, *Neuenfels*, was turned over to the navy in September 1921 for conversion to a seaplane/balloon vessel.

The reconstruction began in December 1921 at Talleres Nuevo Vulcano, Barcelona, to the design of a well-known naval architect, Jacinto Vez, assisted on the aeronautical side by a naval aviator, Capitán de Corbeta Pedro Carona. Upon completion of the main body of work on 1 May 1922, *Dédalo*, as the ship had

Dédalo with one of the SCA airships attached to the mooring mast and carrying Savoia and Macchi flying boats. *Spanish Navy via Michael Burgess*

Dédalo with Savoia and Macchi flying boats on deck and the forward well covered. The large windsock was an unusual feature of the vessel. *Courtesy of Juan Arraez Carda via Georg von Rauch*

been named in honour of the legendary inventor of human flight, finished fitting out, including installation of armament, at Cartagena and was commissioned under the classification of seaplane transport (*transporte de hidroaviones*).

Her aircraft were accommodated on a large aft upper deck; a hangar deck, below, housed hydrogen generation and compression equipment for two kite balloons. The two decks were connected by a large lift just aft of the midships superstructure and the aircraft were handled by booms on two parallel masts forward of the list.

Dédalo's unique feature was a tall airship mooring mast, fitted with a searchlight platform, far forward at the bow, for use by two small semi-rigid airships, the SCA.1 and SCA.2, which were 130ft (42.7m) long with a gas volume of 53,000cu ft. Built by Stabilimento Construzioni Aeronautica in Italy, they were purchased for the Spanish navy in 1922, apparently with their use by *Dédalo* in mind. Aft of the mooring mast was a forecastle well on which an airship could alight atop a system of girders.

Shortly after her commissioning, *Dédalo*, together with the permanently berthed ancient cruiser *Rio de*

la Plata and equally aged destroyer Audaz as depot ships, formed a unit designated Division Naval Aeronautica, based at Barcelona. For the next few years she took part in a number of cruises and exercises, including a fleet visit to Italy in November 1923.

Dédalo's original air complement consisted of Italian Savoia S.16 and Macchi M.18 flying boats. In 1924, these were replaced or supplemented by twelve British Supermarine Scarab amphibian flying boats, embarked by Dédalo at Southampton.

On 3 September 1925, Dédalo accompanied the fleet that landed troops at Alhucemas Bay in Morocco to begin the Franco-Spanish suppression of Abd el Krim's 'Republic of the Riff'. Her aircraft – and, apparently, at least one of the airships – were active in support of land operations leading to the capture of Ajir on 2 October, flying numerous reconnaissance and bombing missions.

This work, however, was severely hampered by bad weather; some cf the aircraft were lost in a storm, and Dédalo herself sustained storm damage. The campaign pointed up the difficulties of operating aircraft from a ship lacking flight deck or catapult, and by the end of the decade Dédalo was obsolete in the face of foreign carrier development. Consequently, she was largely inactive during the early 1930s, except for being part of an interesting experiment on 7 March 1934, when Juan de la Cierva, inventor of the Autogiro, landed on and took off from her deck in one of his craft.

Shortly afterwards, the decision was made to scrap the vessel, but nothing had been done by the outbreak of civil war in mid-1936. Dédalo remained in Republican hands but was inactive during the entire conflict, tied up at Sangunto, where she was damaged by Nationalist aircraft and where she was taken over by Nationalist forces on 29 March 1939. Some months after the end of the war, she was towed to Valencia for scrapping, but before much work had been done she broke in two, possibly as a result of the bomb damage, and sank. The wreck was blown up to clear the harbour, and Dédalo was officially stricken on 1 March 1940.

Dédalo shared with the US Navy oiler Patoka the

A Supermarine Scarab, still bearing British civil registration letters, just before or during transfer of ownership to Spain for use on Dédalo. In the Scarab's unusual configuration, the gunner's position was behind the pilot's cockpit. *Author's collection*

Dédalo's forward well, looking astern. The unusual device on the funnel is believed to be a spark arrester. The two lorries seen at the right were embarked for use ashore with the lighter-than-air craft. *Courtesy of Juan Arraez Carda via Georg von Rauch*

distinction of being the only ships ever fitted with airship mooring masts.

Sweden

Aviation came relatively late to the Royal Swedish Navy, which acquired its first seaplane in 1913 but did not create a real air arm until after World War I and did not assign a surface ship to aviation service until 1929. Years earlier, however, it had been the only navy to possess a balloon boat which, though simply a barge, was the first surface craft specifically built for aeronautical purposes.

Swedish *Ballondepotfartyg Nr 1*, the first vessel to be built specifically for aeronautical purposes, lofting its kite balloon in the typical nose-up attitude of these craft. *Courtesy of Staten Sjöhistoriska Museum, Stockholm*

BALLONDEPOTFARTYG Nr 1 (Balloon Depot Ship No 1)

Displacement:	220t (223.5 tonnes)
Dimensions	154ft × 33ft × 6ft
	(46.8m × 10m × 1.8m)
Aircraft arrangements:	hydrogen generator and compressor, balloon winch; 1 balloon
Complement:	25

Name	Builder	Laid down	Launched	Completed	Fate
BALLONDEPOT-FARTYG Nr 1	Lindholmens Makaniska Verkstad, Gothenburg	1902	17.9.1902	1904	Stricken, 1929, probably BU

This vessel seems to have been quite well designed for its purpose. It was equipped with two petrol engines powering electric generators which operated the hydrogen generation and compression equipment. Its balloon was a German-manufactured Riediger kite balloon of 25,000cu ft hydrogen capacity. It did not prove successful in service, however, probably because it lacked independent mobility, and was transferred to coastal defence forces in 1915. It conducted annual exercises until stricken in 1929.

United States of America

The first US warship to embark on any kind of heavier-than-air flying machine was the torpedo boat *Bagley*, lent to a Massachusetts congressman, Butler Ames, for static tests of a craft of his design, in which lifting power was to be imparted by the rotation of two large drums. A wooden platform was erected over the forecastle to accommodate the machine for tests conducted in July and August 1910. The navy assigned technical observers to the tests, in the belief the device was some sort of man-lifting kite and which proved only that it was incapable of flight.

A more formal but only marginally official introduction of aviation into the US Navy came the next month, when on 26 September Captain Washington I Chambers was designated as the person in the Navy Department to whom correspondence about aviation should be addressed. He was selected for his general technical expertise, but quickly became an enthusiastic exponent of aircraft for naval use.

The platform erected on *Bagley* for tests of the Butler Ames flying machine in 1910. The machine was suspended from the uprights for static tests of its lifting power. *National Archives*

Birmingham with Curtiss pusher on her launching platform shortly before the first takeoff of an aircraft from a surface vessel, 14 November 1910. *National Archives*

Eugene Ely taking the Curtiss pusher off *Birmingham*'s platform, 14 November 1910. Moments after this photo was taken the aircraft brushed the water, damaging the propeller, but Ely landed safely ashore. *National Archives*

Pennsylvania at Mare Island Naval Shipyard in January 1911, fitting out for the landing experiment. The platform and the canvas crash barrier have been installed, but the arresting ropes have not yet been fitted. *National Archives*

It was at Chambers' instigation that two well-known experiments in shipboard takeoff and landing were made. In the first, Eugene Ely, a volunteer civilian aviator, flew a Curtiss pusher biplane off an 83ft (25.3m) × 24ft (7.2m) wooden platform on the forecastle of the scout cruiser *Birmingham* while she was anchored in Hampton Roads on 14 November 1910. For the landing experiment, a wooden platform measuring 119ft 4in (36.3m) × 31ft 6in (9.6m) was constructed over the quarterdeck of the armoured cruiser *Pennsylvania* at the Mare Island Naval Shipyard. A primitive form of arresting gear was installed, in the form of twenty-two athwartship ropes suspended slightly above the platform and weighted at each end by sandbags. Should this fail, a crash barrier was created by stretching a deck awning from the lower mainmast to the fore end of the platform.

Ely, again flying a Curtiss pusher, landed on the platform on 18 January 1911 while the cruiser was anchored in San Francisco Bay. Hooks on the plane's landing gear axle engaged the eleventh line and brought the craft to a halt within 50ft of touchdown. The lines were then removed and Ely flew off from the platform.

This event has often been hailed as the birth of the aircraft carrier, but was, in fact, very much of an artificial setpiece. The arresting gear, while identical in basic principle to that used to this day, was quite impractical for use under service conditions, requiring years of refinement to become a workable proposition, and an adequate flight deck meant development of a radically new type of naval vessel.

The Curtiss pusher flown by Eugene Ely within inches of touching down on *Pennsylvania*'s platform in San Francisco Bay, 18 January 1911, the first landing of an aircraft on a surface vessel. Deck awnings spread from both sides of the platform were safety devices intended to ensure that if the aircraft swerved it would fall cleanly into the water and not strike deck gear. *National Archives*

Neither was undertaken by the US Navy for several years, despite various unofficial recommendations and proposals for aviation vessels, some envisioning a clear flight deck. The only other aircraft platform to be seen on a US warship until late in World War I was erected on a destroyer, USS *Paulding*, the same month as Ely's landing. About 70ft (23m) long, it was installed for possible assistance to a civilian aviator, John A D McCurdy, in a flight from Key West, Florida, to Havana. It was fitted with a hinged extension that could be lowered to sea level, the idea being that if McCurdy were forced down, and his plane remained afloat, it would be hauled onto the platform for takeoff. This was exactly what happened, on 31 January 1911, but the Curtiss pusher was so badly damaged during its recovery that takeoff was impossible.

On the same day that McCurdy came to grief, *Pennsylvania*, with the platform removed, was conducting the US Navy's only experiment with lofting a man-lifting kite; she then steamed into San Diego harbour where, on 17 February, pioneer aeronautical engineer and aviator Glenn Curtiss flew a prototype seaplane out to her.

The craft was hoisted aboard by a boat crane and, after a brief stay, was lowered to the water for a return flight. This simple event was a significant landmark in the development of shipboard aviation; it demonstrated for the first time that a seaplane could be handled by a surface vessel.

It also reinforced Chambers' belief that seagoing aircraft should not be concentrated on special vessels, which he dismissed as 'floating garages', but could and should become standard items of equipment aboard regular warships. To this

The successful conclusion of the first shipboard landing. Ely, second from left in the foreground wearing a helmet, has just alighted from the Curtiss. Sandbags to left and right have been displaced by the engagement of hooks in the aircraft's axle with their connecting lines. *National, Archives*

A Curtiss AB-2 flying boat on *North Carolina*'s first catapult, 6 november 1915, at Pensacola shortly
before it became the first aircraft to be launched from a shipboard catapult. The port 10in gun has
been made into an improvised hoist, by the insertion of a boat boom. *National Archives*

end, he inaugurated development of the catapult as a faster and more reliable way of
getting an aircraft aloft than lowering it for a water takeoff. The motive power was
to be compressed air, available on all ships mounting torpedo tubes. The first
catapult was a failure when tested ashore on 31 July 1912, badly damaging the test
aircraft. An improved version, mounted on a barge at the Washington Navy Yard,
successfully launched a floatplane on 12 November 1912 and the next month
launched the US Navy's first flying boat.

Matters rested there for nearly three years, but the potential value of such a
catapult was shown when US naval aircraft were first employed in quasi-combat
during the occupation of Vera Cruz, Mexico, in April 1914. A floatplane and a flying
boat were taken there on the battleship *Mississippi*, and on 25 April the flying boat

The improved and raised catapult being installed on *North Carolina* at Pensacola, 17 May 1916. This view illustrates
how the catapult restricted training of the aft turret, whose guns here are pointed to the port quarter. *National Archives*

made two reconnaissance flights, lowered to the water and recovered by improvised hoists. This proved so cumbersome that both aircraft were transferred ashore.

Chambers had been eased out of aviation work before the first US Navy air department, the Bureau of Aeronautics, was established on 1 July 1914, but interest in the catapult revived. An improved model, mounted on *Navy Coal Barge No 214* at Pensacola, Florida, the US Navy's first air station, was tested successfully in early 1915 and launched an aircraft for the first time on 16 April. In late October, it was placed aboard the armoured cruiser *North Carolina*, the air station's base ship, fitted about four feet above the quarterdeck to launch over the stern. In the absence of any shipboard gear able to handle aircraft, a hoist was improvised by inserting a boat boom in the muzzle of the aft turret's portside 10in gun. On 5 November, *North Carolina* launched a Curtiss flying boat. Two more successful launches were made but a crash on the next attempt caused the tests to be suspended.

Installation of a further improved catapult on the cruiser began in April 1916. At 103ft it was about twice as long as the earlier version and was raised to boat-deck level by 14ft stanchions, running from the base of the mainmast to the stern over the aft turret. It was connected to parallel port and starboard tracks curving about the

This view of *North Carolina* shows the contrast between the first catapult installation and the raised one. The Curtiss AB.3 flying boat is on the catapult and the starboard boat crane shows the extension fitted to it for aircraft handling. *National Archives*

The Curtiss AB.3 flying boat, piloted by Godfrey de C Chevalier, airborne after the first underway catapult launching from *North Carolina*, 12 July 1916. *National Archives*

mainmast, which permitted carriage of up to five aircraft. The hoisting problem was solved by fitting 40ft extensions to the boat cranes. On 12 July, the catapult shot off a Curtiss flying boat in the first under-way launching.

Similar catapults and boat crane extensions were installed on two more armoured cruisers during refits in early 1917 – *Huntington*, a sister of *Pennsylvania*, at Mare Island, and *Seattle* (ex-*Washington*, the name having been changed during the refit), a sister of *North Carolina*, at Portsmouth. A fourth ship, *Montana*, was also scheduled to be fitted, to form a complete division of 'catapult cruisers', but work never got beyond the preliminary stage.

The three cruisers exercised their aircraft more or less successfully for a few months in 1917. The Curtiss pusher seaplanes that had been used in the early catapult trials were now hopelessly obsolete by European standards, and the cruisers carried three tractor-engine types – the twin-float Curtiss R.6 and the single-float Curtiss N.9 and Thomas-Morse SH.4. In June, *Huntington*, which replaced *North Carolina* at the Pensacola air base, experimentally lofted and towed a kite balloon for the first time in the US Navy.

Seattle had a catapult aboard for the shortest time, from her recommissioning on 31 March 1917 until June when she was being made ready at Brooklyn for Atlantic convoy escort duty. *North Carolina*'s catapult was also removed in 1917, but the exact date is not known.

Huntington retained her catapult during her first Atlantic convoy cruise in September 1917 but the aircraft were struck below. She also retained the balloon, but it was blown away in bad weather on 17 September; a shipfitter won the war's first Medal of Honour by rescuing the balloonist. When *Huntington* returned to home waters in October, the catapult was removed at Brooklyn.

Removal of the catapults has sometimes been criticized as a retrogressive step. But, in fact, they and their aircraft were useless for the sort of service the cruisers were called upon to perform. The seaplanes could not be sheltered against bad weather, nor could they be launched or recovered during unfavourable conditions. Lacking

A view of *Huntington*, taken from her kite balloon, off Pensacola on 2 June 1917 as she prepared to launch a Curtiss N.9H from her catapult. The balloon mooring line can be seen extending from the mainmast. *National Archives*

Armoured cruiser *Huntington* lofting an early kite balloon at Pensacola, 23 June 1917. A Curtiss N.9H is aboard and another seaplane is in the air at the right. *National Archives*

A blurred photograph of *Huntington*, taken moments after that on p 113, shows the seaplane leaving the catapult. *National Archives*

armament and wireless, the seaplanes could do little in the way of convoy protection. Added to which, they would have made the cruisers excellent U-boat targets when the ships hove to for recovery. The catapults restricted training arcs of the aft turrets, making fire dead astern impossible.

Little more was done in practical US Navy aviation vessel development during World War I, but *Huntington*'s balloon re-established a US naval-aeronautical link, broken more than half a century earlier.

FANNY

Machinery:	steam engine, 1 shaft
Armament:	1–32pdr, 1–8pdr
Complement:	49
No other details known	

It is impossible to trace the origins of this single-crew steamship, which entered service with the US Union Army (not Navy) sometime in 1861 as a gunboat-cum-transport. She is the first surface vessel known to have lofted a captive manned balloon, when, on 3 August 1861, a civilian aeronaut, John La Mountain, ascended from her deck to observe Confederate army positions on the shores of Hampton Roads, Virginia. He made a second ascent a few days later, from either *Fanny* or a ship named *Adriatic*, which could have been any one of five steam vessels of that name in US registry in 1861.

The only other Union steam vessel known to have operated a balloon during the civil war was a ship from which another civilian aeronaut, John B Starkweather, made a series of ascents in April 1862 at Port Royal, South Carolina. Its name is usually given as *Mayflower*, but it is far more likely to have been *May Flower*, a 262-ton, 133-foot sidewheel paddle steamer built in New York in 1845 and reconstructed in 1859.

Fanny was captured by Confederate gunboats in an engagement off Roanoke Island, Virginia, on 1 October 1861 and taken into Confederate service without change of name. Engaged by Union vessels on 10 February 1862 at Elizabeth City, North Carolina, she was run aground and blown up to avoid capture. *May Flower* was lost, listed as burned, in October 1872.

An artist's depiction of *Fanny*, the first vessel to employ a manned captive balloon, under attack by Confederate ships just before her capture on 1 October 1861. *Reproduction from an engraving in* Leslie's Weekly, *author's collection*

A well-known model of *George Washington Parke Custis*, the most accurate known depiction of the craft. Hydrogen generation and purification apparatus forward, spherical balloon amidships and deckhouse aft. *Courtesy of Mariners Museum, Newport News, Va.*

GEORGE WASHINGTON PARKE CUSTIS

Dimensions:	122ft × 14ft 6in × 5ft 6in
	(37m × 4.4m × 1.7m)
Carrying capacity:	75 to 120t (87 to 139 tonnes)

Purchased for $150 in August 1861 for use as a coal barge at the Washington, DC, Navy Yard, this nondescript craft became the first surface vessel to be specifically configured for operation of an aerial device. She was assigned to Thaddeus S C Lowe, civilian chief of the Union Army's amorphous balloon corps, in response to his request for a craft to provide greater mobility between balloon posts on the Potomac River.

The vessel was modified at the Washington Navy Yard, under Lowe's supervision, with the addition of an ellipsoid flush deck and the installation of hydrogen generating equipment and a deckhouse. The work was completed in early November 1861 and on 10 November the boat, towed by the sidewheel steamer *Coeur de Lion* and with a detachment of infantrymen to handle the balloon lines, sailed on her first mission, a reconnaissance of Confederate positions along the Potomac.

The boat operated on the Potomac during late 1861 and early 1862, towed by a variety of ships. From late March to early May 1862 she operated on the York River during the Peninsula campaign. In August 1862, she was assigned to observe the results of a Union squadron's bombardment of the Confederate Fort Powhatan. Towed by steam tug *Stepping Stones*, she joined sloop *Wachusett*, gunboats *Tioga* and *Port Royal* and armed transport *Delaware* in what has been called (with exaggeration but some truth) 'the first carrier task force'. Unfortunately, the results of this action are not known.

An even more unusual and historic use of a balloon from a floating platform occurred in late March 1862 when civilian aeronaut John H Steiner took aloft, from an unnamed flatboat in the Mississippi River, naval officers whose aerial observation enabled Union mortar boats to fire more accurately at a Confederate stronghold called Island No 10. Aerial guidance of naval gunfire would not be repeated in wartime for nearly a half century.

Highly indirectly and at a far remove in time and geography, Steiner was to prove an influence on the development of the aircraft carrier. In August 1863, he gave a balloon ascent to a young German army officer, Count Ferdinand von Zeppelin, attached to the Union Army as a military observer. Many years later, Zeppelin revealed that this flight was the germ of his inspiration to create the rigid airship, the craft that so strongly influenced the Royal Navy's development of shipboard aviation during 1914–18.

Steiner was no longer in army service when he met Zeppelin, for the Union balloon corps, never appreciated by officialdom, was disbanded – or, more properly, simply fell apart – in early 1863. With its demise, *George Washington Parke Custis* was returned to the Washington Navy Yard, her fate remaining unknown.

Revival of interest

More than half a century elapsed before the next proposal for converting a surface craft for aeronautical purposes was given official and serious consideration in the United States. It was the result of a recommendation to the Secretary of the Navy on 26 March 1917 from Lieutenant (later Captain) Kenneth Whiting, then in charge of the seaplane contingent on *Seattle* and later an influential figure in the development of US Navy shipboard aviation. Whiting recommended that a vessel be acquired to ascertain what types of seaplanes were best suited for fleet use, 'by trying under actual conditions those that appear to have the necessary desirable qualifications'.

Whiting thought that one of the rail ferries operated by the Florida East Coast Railway Company between Key West, Florida, and Havana would be a good choice for such a ship. They measured 336ft 8in (110m) × 59ft (19.4m) × 18ft 8in (6.1m) and made 15kts. Citing their commodiousness, he stated, 'The entire main deck is available for stowing seaplanes where they would be protected from the weather – seaplanes of all types up to 80 feet span could be accommodated. The upper deck aft of the smokestacks can be made available for landing tests. A catapult could be installed on the main deck aft, for launching seaplanes'. This vessel 'could accompany supply ships patrolling with the [Atlantic Fleet] Destroyer Force and hence aviators would always be available for protective scouting, patrolling in vicinity of Fleet's base, etc., while valuable experience would be gained daily'.

Whiting's proposal gained unanimously favourable endorsements as it was circulated through US Navy bureaux, including one from the Destroyer Force's commanding officer, but was eventually scotched on 20 June 1917 by the Bureau of Steam Engineering and the General Board because '... the present supply of seaplanes and aviators is inadequate, and ... the seaplanes themselves are in need of further development, it is not recommended that this ship be taken over for such work. It is considered that the Navy's seaplane development could be pushed with greater success from an experimental station on shore'. The ship referred to was one of the rail ferries, the 2699-ton *Henry M. Flagler*, which Whiting had mentioned in passing in his March memo but not had specifically recommended for purchase. The General Board apparently assumed that he had. The rejection document also refers to a forward installation a catapult, whereas Whiting had suggested aft placement.

Meanwhile, the United States had entered World War I, and fifteen days before Whiting's proposal was rejected, he had landed in France as commander of the US Navy's First Aeronautic Detachment – the first US military unit to arrive in Europe – from the collier *Jupiter*, the vessel that not many years later would become the US Navy's first flight deck carrier.

Whiting returned to the subject in August 1918, urging construction of two seaplane carriers to attack from the North Sea German naval bases that were beyond the range of land-based US aircraft, but nothing came of the proposal. However, as the potential of shipboard aviation was increasingly realized in the light of wartime experience, pressure built for an American carrier of some type or another.

Preliminary US Navy thoughts about a carrier were

A Hickman-Mustin Sea Sled with a Caproni
Ca.5 bomber aboard at Hampton Roads, about
November 1918. A Curtiss flying boat, probably
an F.5L, is in the background. *National Archives*

strongly influenced by a British naval architect, S V
Goodall (later the Royal Navy's Director of Naval
Construction), who was seconded to the Bureau of
Construction and Repair in 1917, and imparted his
ideas on aviation vessels to his American collabor-
ators. Goodall believed the salient characteristics of
a carrier should be high speed to permit work with
scouting forces, strong anti-torpedo protection, arm-
our of light cruiser standard, and a heavy anti-aircraft

and torpedo armament.

Most of these features appeared in a design presented to the General Board in June 1918 by Captain
Noble E Irwin, Director of Naval Aeronautics, for a
15,000-ton ship, 700ft × 80ft, with a speed of 30kts, a
single lift and an exclusively AA armament. The design
was flawed by that recurring theme in early carrier
theory, an athwartship structure, in this case a girder-
supported bridge spanning the flight deck. When this

Shawmut at Guantanamo Bay in January 1930.
A Curtiss N.9H is moored to her stern, and the
empennage of another can be seen on deck.
National Archives

feature came under criticism later, in the light of British experience, Irwin altered the scheme to provide an offset island-type superstructure.

Before that, however, the General Board, under pressure from Admiral William Sims, commander of US Navy forces in Europe, for a carrier, recommended construction of six ships along the lines of Irwin's original design. The recommendation was rejected by the Secretary of the Navy Josephus Daniels in October 1918, on the grounds that the vessels could not be completed before the end of the war.

Consequently, the only craft that might be termed an aviation vessel produced by the United States during World War I was the brainstorm of another early and influential naval aviator, Commander (later Captain) Henry C Mustin. In early 1918, impressed with the British use of towed aircraft-carrying lighters, Mustin suggested a powered version based on a high-speed planing hull developed in 1911 by W Albert Hickman, from which an aeroplane could take off. He advocated construction of no fewer than 5600 such vessels, to carry three different types of aircraft for a massive attack on northern Germany from off the Dutch coast. Such a figure, he believed, was within American industrial capacity, although it has been aptly noted that it was 'regarded by many as preposterous'.

Preposterous or not, the idea attracted enough support for Mustin to be assigned to the Bureau of Construction and Repair to supervise a construction and trials programme for the craft, which became known as the Hickman-Mustin Sea Sled. Displacing 25t (25.4tonnes) with a length of 55ft (16.7m), it was powered by four petrol engines producing a total of 1800hp for a designed speed of 47 knots (slightly exceeded in trials).

The first Sea Sled was delivered at Boston in September 1918 and ran trials with an Italian trimotor Caproni Ca.5 bomber aboard, although it is not known whether a takeoff was attempted or achieved. The armistice ended the construction programme but trials continued and, on 7 March 1919, a Curtiss R.9 took off from a Sea Sled at Hampton Roads. The few units completed subsequently were used as rescue boats, work for which their high speed suited them admirably.

In the immediate postwar years, the only US Navy aviation vessels of sorts were two converted ships.

SHAWMUT

Displacement:	3746t (3806 tonnes) standard
Dimensions:	386ft oa × 52ft 2in × 15ft 7in
	(126.9m × 17.1m × 5.1m)
Machinery:	vertical triple expansion, 8 boilers, 2 shafts, 7000ihp = 14kts. Coal: 400t (448.2 tonnes).
	Oil: 160t (162.5 tonnes)
Armament:	1–5in/51 (127mm) LA, 2–3in/50 (76.2mm) AA, 2 MG; after May 1943 1–5in, 4–3in AA, 4–40mm
	AA, 8–20mm AA; 300 mines
Aircraft arrangements:	2 seaplane booms on kingposts, hydrogen generator, 2 hydrogen compressors
Complement:	344

Name	Builder	Laid down	Launched	Completed	Fate
SHAWMUT, ex-MASSACHUSETTS	William Cramp & Sons Ship & Engine Company, Philadelphia	?	1907	1907	BU, 1965

Massachusetts of the Eastern Steamship Company was purchased by the navy on 12 November 1917 and converted to a minelayer at the Boston Navy Yard, commissioned on 7 December 1917, and renamed *Shawmut* on 7 January 1918. She arrived in European waters in June 1918 and helped lay the North Sea mine barrage.

On 27 January 1919 *Shawmut* was selected to become a temporary tender, repair vessel and accommodation ship for an aviation detachment assigned to the Atlantic Fleet at Guantanamo Bay, Cuba. She was converted at the Boston Navy yard by removal of her mine rails, some other mining equipment and aft gun, and installation of aircraft repair equipment, fuel stowage space, seaplane-handling booms, additional accommodation, a hydrogen generator and two hydrogen compressors. Arriving at Guantanamo on 14 February 1919, she was responsible for tending five Curtiss H.16 flying boats and inflating and maintaining six kite balloons for use by battleships. She continued this duty until early April, and in May was detached to support the transatlantic flight of Navy NC flying boats. She continued aviation service with the Atlantic Fleet until 1 January 1928, when she reverted to mine service, renamed *Oglala*, as flagship of Mine Division 1.

Oglala was sunk by Japanese aircraft at Pearl Harbour, Hawaii, on 7 December 1941, raised in 1942, repaired at Mare Island Naval Shipyard and recommissioned on 21 May 1943 as a miscellaneous repair ship (ARG 1) with increased armament. She served in the Pacific until the end of World War II, was stricken on 11 July 1946 and transferred to the Maritime Commission. She was the depot ship for the Reserve Fleet at Benicia, California, until scrapped in 1965.

Aroostook at Colo Solo, Panama Canal Zone, in March 1930, before she ended aviation service. *Author's collection*

AROOSTOOK

Displacement:	3800t (3861 tonnes) standard
Dimensions:	395ft × 52ft 2in × 16ft
	(129.9 × 17.1m × 5.2m)
Machinery:	vertical triple expansion, 8 boilers, 2 shafts, 7000ihp = 20kts
Armament:	1–5in/51 (127mm) LA, 2–3in/50 (76.2mm) AA, 2 MG; 300 mines
Aircraft arrangements:	2 seaplane booms on kingposts, stowage for 5000 gallons of aircraft fuel
Complement:	314 to 367

Name	Builder	Laid down	Launched	Completed	Fate
AROOSTOOK, ex-BUNKER HILL	William Cramp & Sons Ship & Engine Company, Philadelphia	?	1907	1907	BU, 1948

The Eastern Steamship Company's *Bunker Hill*, a near sister of *Massachusetts/Shawmut*, was purchased at the same time and underwent the same conversion to a minelayer at the Boston Navy Yard. She was commissioned on 7 December 1917, and, from June 1918, helped to lay the North Sea mine barrage. In 1919, she was assigned to support the NC flight and in May brought home from Lisbon the NC.4, the only one of the flying boats to complete the crossing.

In early 1920, she was assigned as an aircraft tender with the Pacific Fleet, being converted in the same manner as *Shawmut* at the Mare Island Naval Ship-yard with the exception that no balloon equipment was installed. The aviation service was intended to last no more than eighteen months but, in the absence of any other suitable ship, she continued in the role for several years. In September 1925, she supported the California-to-Hawaii flight of the Navy PN.9 flying boat and, in January 1929, she substituted for the carrier *Langley* in war games which took place around the Panama Canal, operating a single Sikorsky amphibious flying boat to represent the carrier's air group.

During war games in 1931, *Aroostook* supported aircraft practising dive bombing of radio-controlled target destroyers. That was her last aviation duty; she was decommissioned on 10 March 1931 and never re-entered naval service although designated a cargo ship (AK 44) on 20 May 1941. Transferred to the Maritime Commission on 5 February 1943, she was sold after the war, and her hulk became a floating gambling casino at Long Beach, California, named *Lux*. When that use was finally prohibited by law, the hulk was scrapped in 1948.

In spite of their long association with aviation, neither *Aroostook* nor *Shawmut* was ever rated as an aviation vessel but retained the minelayer designations of CM 3 and CM 4, respectively, that they were given in 1920. Both were expected to return to mine service eventually, and for that reason not all their minelaying equipment was removed. Neither was a satisfactory aircraft tender, for reasons pointed out in 1931 when *Oglala* was considered for reversion to that role as a seaplane depot ship at Pearl Harbour: they were overcrowded, their wooden structure constituted a fire hazard when aircraft fuel was carried, deck space was inadequate for aircraft accommodation, and their short roll periods made hoisting of seaplanes dang-

erous except in calm water. Nevertheless, they rendered valuable service during a period when superior ships were lacking.

Wright in her original configuration as a lighter-than-air tender at Hampton Roads, 2 October 1922, pending conversion to a seaplane tender. The aft balloon well is covered over. *National Archives*

WRIGHT (AZ 1, AV 1, AG 79)

Displacement:	8675t (8814.4 tonnes) full load
Dimensions:	448ft oa × 58ft 3in × 27ft (maximum)
	(136.5m × 17.7m × 8.2m)
Machinery:	geared turbines, 6 boilers, 1 shaft, 6000shp = 15kts. Oil: 1629t (1655 tonnes)
Armament:	2–5in/51 (127mm) LA 2 × 1, 2–3in/50 (76.2m) AA 2 × 1, 4 MG
Aircraft arrangements:	balloon well as completed, accommodation for 12 aircraft, aircraft repair and maintenance equipment, aircraft fuel stowage
Complement:	311–350

Name	Builder	Laid down	Launched	Completed	Fate
WRIGHT, ex-SOMME	American International Shipbuilding Corporation, Hog Island, Tiegen & Land Dry Dock Company, Hoboken	1919	28.4.1920	16.12.1921	BU, 1948

After an inauspicious venture into lighter-than-air aeronautics in 1915–16, the US Navy followed the lead of its wartime allies and established an LTA arm that included, as well as airships, kite balloons to be towed by warships. By the armistice, at least four battleships and six destroyers had operated balloons. This experience led to a postwar decision to fit out balloon ships along the British model.

There were to have been three such ships, and to expedite their introduction into service they were to be completed from a group of eleven incomplete hulls under construction at Hog Island, Pennsylvania, as army transports. Hulls Nos 675, 678 and 680 were selected. But when the navy board assigned to redesign them inspected the work, it found that Nos 675 and 678 were at such an advanced stage of construction that to rebuild them to balloon ship specifications would have been prohibitively expensive. The reason for the error in assigning them was never explained, but the upshot was that after a great deal of discussion, the navy settled upon the only usable hull, No 680, which was to have been named *Somme* (a name reassigned to one of the other transports).

Officially acquired by the navy on 30 June 1920, the incomplete vessel was transferred to Tiegen & Land Dry Dock Company in Hoboken, New Jersey, where she was finished as a balloon ship, renamed *Wright* in honour of the American aeronautical pioneers and designed AZ 1 – the only US ship to bear the nomenclature code for 'lighter-than-air craft tender'.

Although also equipped for tending seaplanes, *Wright's* main aeronautical feature upon completion was a large aft balloon well, with mooring equipment at the stern. Experiments with balloon operation were carried out during a cruise in the Caribbean shortly after her commissioning. Practically as soon as she had entered service, however, the navy decided to end the use of shipboard balloons. This was due partly to a series of accidents with them, but more importantly because it had been found during fleet manoeuvres that their chief function, spotting for ships' gunfire, could be performed more efficiently and effectively by aircraft.

As a result, *Wright* flew her balloon for the last time on 16 July 1922 at Hampton Roads. She was rebuilt as a seaplane tender, with the balloon well decked over, redesignated AV 1 on 11 November 1923. As such, she had a nominal capacity of twelve floatplanes but during the 1920s and '30s functioned primarily as a mother ship for patrol flying boats, sometimes tending as many as thirty-two. As the largest, best-equipped vessel of her type (the others being imperfectly converted colliers, destroyers, minelayers, minesweepers and Eagle boats), and fitted as a flagship, *Wright* performed valuable service in perfecting the operation of the patrol squadrons.

During 1939–41, she installed aviation units on US Pacific islands, including the ill-fated one on Wake. After 7 December 1941, she operated extensively throughout the Pacific, steaming thousands upon thousands of miles to dozens of ports and islands, largely as a transport conveying all manner of men and *matériel*, but continuing to tend seaplanes from time to time. By late 1944, with purpose-built seaplane tenders coming into US Navy service in large numbers, her aviation role was diminished and she was relegated entirely to cargo carrying, redesignated a miscellaneous auxiliary (AG 79) on 1 October 1944 and renamed *San Clemente* on 1 Febrary 1945.

Worn from years of hard service, she was decommissioned on 21 June 1946, stricken on 1 July 1946, transferred to the Maritime Commission on 21 September 1946 and sold for scrapping on 19 August 1948.

Meanwhile, back at the Bureau of Construction and Repair, work on flight-deck carrier design had continued. A plan advanced in October 1918 called for a ship of around 24,000 tons, a length of 800ft and a speed of 35 knots, featuring dual parallel superstructures. In early 1919, a vessel about 10,000 tons heavier was proposed, still with dual superstructure.

Thought was also given to conversion of three merchant ships, the medium-sized *Charles* and *Yale* that had served as cross-Channel transports for the American Expeditionary Force and the larger *Mount Vernon*, a former German liner that had been interned early in the war, seized in 1917 and used as a transatlantic troop transport.

The conversions foundered because of technical difficulties and cost, and construction of a new ship was barred by the refusal of Congress to approve funds for carriers in the 1920/21 fiscal year naval appropriations.

The problems involved in conversion of large merchant ships, such as liners, were well set forth in a memorandum of 29 January 1921, by Naval Constructor Jerome C Hunsaker. He was responding to a plan presented to the House of Representatives' Military Affairs Committee by Brigadier General William Mitchell, the single-minded air-power advocate, for reconstruction into carriers of the liners *Agamemnon* (ex-*Kaiser Wilhelm II*), *Von Steuben* (ex-*Kronprinz Wilhelm*) and *Leviathan* (ex-*Kronprinzessin Cecilie*), the latter a giant of more than 54,000 tons. All, like *Mount Vernon*, had been interned, seized and used as troop transports. The memo is worth quoting at length:

> Passenger vessels… do not lend themselves for conversion to satisfactory airplane carriers as a large portion of the ship must be cut down and new structure built so as to provide stowage spaces for the airplanes and space for elevators to bring them up on deck and to provide an entirely flush deck above everything. The ex-German ships named have enormous upper works and a large portion of the ship is taken up with the machinery and boiler spaces, etc. Also these vessels are coal burning which makes it a serious problem to devise means of disposing elsewhere of large volumes of smoke which pour out of the large smoke-stacks when the vessel is running at high speed

Hunsaker also pointed out that the liners were totally devoid of protection against shellfire and bombs and were especially vulnerable to torpedoes. As for *Leviathan*, her draught was too deep for many harbours, and he estimated the cost of her conversion would run to more than $10,000,000.

A breakthrough was finally made as the result of hearings in March and April 1919 by the General Board to sound out the whole matter of carriers. A case for conversion of a collier was made to the Board by Whiting, who was now a commander and an assistant to the Director of Naval Aeronautics. He – and practically everybody else – would have preferred construction but, in the face of unwillingness of Congress to finance such a ship, was prepared to accept a less capable vessel with which trials could be conducted until the pursestrings were loosened.

Whiting's suggestion of a collier was based on a number of considerations, some of which one can assume stemmed from his experience on *Jupiter*. The configuration of a collier lent itself to carrier structure. Its length was sufficient for a flight deck, its capacious holds could easily accommodate aircraft, the aft location of the machinery promised to simplify the problem of venting engine room gases with a minimum of disturbance to flight operations, and the manning requirements (exclusive of aviation personnel) were minimal. The latter was an important consideration at a time when the US Navy was discharging the large number of men it had enlisted during the war years. Finally, as the navy was becoming increasingly oil-fired, a coal-carrier was the type of ship most likely

to be dispensed with in the near future.

Whiting suggested the collier *Neptune*, which had followed *Jupiter* to France with the rest of the First Aeronautic Detachment; others advocated *Jason*, but the Board finally decided on *Jupiter* because of her slightly higher speed, recommending her conversion by a vote taken on 15 April 1919. After strong representation to Congress, funds were approved for the conversion, in the Naval Appropriations Act of 1920, signed by President Woodrow Wilson on 11 July 1919.

Work on the conversion was, however, delayed, first by the Chief of Naval Operations, Admiral William S Benson, for reasons that are unclear, then by lack of experience in aviation requirements and faulty co-ordination among the three bureaus responsible for the design. It was not until 24 March 1920 that *Jupiter* was decommissioned at the Norfolk Navy Yard for her transformation to begin under the designation CV 1.

LANGLEY (CV 1, AV 3)

Displacement:	13,989t (14,213.8 tonnes) normal, 11,050t (11,227.5 tonnes) standard, 14,700t (14,936 tonnes) full load
Dimensions:	542ft 2in × 65ft 3in × 20ft 6in (mean)
	(166.2m × 20m × 6.1m)
Machinery:	turbine with electric drive, 3 boilers, 2 shafts, 7152shp = 15kts (14.99kts on trials). Oil: 2003t
	(2035 tonnes) 12,260 nm at 10kts
Armament:	4–5in/51 (127mm) LA 4 × 1
Aircraft	
arrangements:	flight deck 523ft (159.4m) × 65ft (19.8m), lift 36ft (10.9m) × 46ft (14m), 2 catapults (originally),
	2 seaplane cranes, interior gantry crane, stowage for 251,000 gallons of aircraft fuel
Complement:	53 as collier, 410 to 468 as carrier

Name	Builder	Laid down	Launched	Completed	Fate
LANGLEY, ex-JUPITER	Mare Island Navy Shipyard, Vallejo	18.10.1911	24.8.1912	7.4.1913	Sunk by Japanese aircraft, 27 February 1942

Jupiter was the US Navy's first turbo-electric powered vessel, a system that permitted her to steam at full speed astern. She was renamed *Langley* on 21 April 1920 during her conversion, the name honouring the famous, albeit unsuccessful, aeronautical pioneer Samuel Pierpont Langley. She was commissioned as a carrier on 20 March 1922.

The wooden flight deck was carried by twenty-six steel truss girders, thirteen on each side, above what had been the collier's upper deck. The first of what had been six coal holds was used for aircraft fuel stowage, the fourth housed the lift and its mechanism, with the magazine below it, and the remaining four accommodated disassembled aircraft that were carried by an overhead gantry crane for assembly on the lift, which in its down position was not flush with the deck but about eight feet above it. Disassembly allowed the vessel to carry a number of aircraft disproportionate to her size; thirty-three became the standard complement and on at least one occasion

she embarked an incredible fifty-five.

The original forward bridge structure was retained, with the flight deck running over it. A single aft portside funnel, hinged for lowering to a horizontal position during flight operations, was cross-connected to a starboard smoke-venting opening below the flight deck on the starboard side which was fitted with a smoke-suppressing device. This system was not a success and was later replaced by two smaller, hinged portside funnels.

Langley originally had one catapult, then another was installed, nearly identical to those on the prewar armoured cruisers; 94 feet long, they could launch a 6000lb (2730kg) aircraft at 55kts. They were soon replaced by improved models, set into the flight deck fore and aft, but these were removed in 1928 after not having been used for three years.

The original flight-deck arresting gear was similar to that of *Argus* and other early British carriers, a combination of fore-and-aft and athwartship wires.

A bow view of *Langley* with her original single portside funnel, 12 September 1922. *Author's collection*

A stern view of *Langley*, 12 September 1922, with the retractable masts raised. The structure on the fantail is the pigeon cote, later the executive officer's cabin. *Author's collection*

A Vought O2U on *Langley*'s flight deck *c*1930. The cross-deck arresting lines are visible and the funnels have been lowered. An interesting comparison can be made with the photograph of *Hosho* on p 89 (bottom). *Author's collection*

This was replaced later by a totally athwartship system of wires connected to braking drums; this eliminated need for hooks on aircraft landing gear axles and is essentially the same type still in use today.

An unusual early feature was a large carrier pigeon cote right aft on the fantail. When pigeon communication was eventually entirely superseded by wireless, this was remodelled into a cabin for the executive officer.

Langley began aircraft deck trials in October 1922, with the first takeoff made on 17 October by Lieutenant Virgil C Griffin in a Vought VE.7SF, and the first landing on 26 October by Lieutenant Commander Godfrey de C Chevalier in an Aeromarine 39.B. The first catapult launch was made on 18 November by Whiting, now *Langley*'s executive officer, in a Naval Aircraft Factory PT.2 floatplane.

In December 1922, *Langley* began to receive her

Langley with her revised two-funnel
arrangement at Balboa, Panama Canal Zone, on
9 June 1930. *Author's collection*

Langley in the Panama Canal's Gatun lock, 3
March 1930. Twenty-four aircraft, her entire
complement at the time, are on deck – eight
Curtiss F6C.4s, eight Boeing F2B-1s and eight
Vought O2Us. *Author's collection*

first standard air complement, squadron VF 1, the
US Navy's first carrier fighter unit, equipped with
the Naval Aircraft Factory/Curtiss TS.1, the first
American naval aircraft designed specifically as a
fighter. From then, until the mid-1930s, she was to
carry a wide assortment of aircraft, both experimental
and standard. In 1927, she is believed to have operated
at least one twin-engine Douglas T2D.1, which would
make her the first carrier to send off a multi-engine

aircraft. On 23 September 1931, she carried out
landing and takeoff trials of a Pitcairn XOP.1 Autogiro, the first by the US Navy of a rotary-wing aircraft.

From the start, *Langley* was regarded as a purely
experimental craft, not a fighting vessel (which is one
reason that her slow speed was acceptable). This status
was given international legal recognition under Article
VIII of the Washington Naval Treaty, which provided
that all aircraft carriers existing or under construction
as of 12 November 1921 should be considered experimental. *Argus* and *Hosho* were also covered by this
clause.

As an experimental craft, the Covered Wagon
(as she was nicknamed because of her appearance)
rendered invaluable service for nearly fourteen years,
helping to pioneer every technique and doctrine of
carrier operation, including development of the carrier
task force concept. By the mid-1930s, however, her
experimental value was at an end and she was decommissioned on 25 October 1936 at the Mare Island
Naval Shipyard for conversion to a seaplane tender,
emerging on 25 February 1937 with the designation
AV 3 and the forward 200ft (60.9m) of her flight deck
removed.

Early in the Pacific war, *Langley* was used as an
aircraft transport. She was sunk by Japanese naval
aircraft, with the loss of sixteen lives, on 27 February
1942 while en route to Tjilatjap, Java, with a cargo
of US Army Curtiss P.40 fighter planes.

Early in her career, *Langley* was indirectly associated with two unusual US Navy shipboard aviation
experiments. In August 1923, some of her personnel
helped install a float-equipped TS.1 on the forecastle
of destroyer *Charles Ausburn* at Norfolk, to test the
feasibility of operating scout planes from such vessels.
Some flights were successfully made, but the aircraft
interfered too much with ship's routine and the idea
was dropped. Ultimately, the US Navy did operate a
few aircraft-equipped destroyers before scrapping the
whole concept as inefficient and superfluous.

Earlier in 1923, *Langley* personnel assisted initially
in the first tests of an aircraft-carrying submarine. The
submarine *S1* was modified at the Portsmouth Navy
Yard to carry a small scouting seaplane. It was to be
launched in the same manner as those of *U12* and
E22, but instead of being carried on deck it was
stowed, disassembled, in a cylindrical pressure-resist-
ant hangar so the boat would not have to remain on
the surface. The hangar was mounted abaft the conning tower, and the vessel was further modified by
slight alteration of the conning tower structure and
removal of the 4in deck gun.

Between late 1923 and late 1926, *S1* carried out
tests with two aircraft of identical design but different
methods of construction, the Martin MS and Cox-
Klemin XS – with long delays between experiments,

while the planes were modified for speedier assembly and disassembly. Underwater carriage, launching and recovery were ultimately quite successful, but the seaplanes proved too underpowered and unseaworthy for practical use. Further tests were carried out in 1931 with a sturdier aircraft, the Leoning XSL flying boat, but the idea was eventually abandoned and the hangar removed from *S1*.

Langley in her final configuration as AV 3 at French Frigate Schoals on 27 October 1937. The original bridge structure is now visible and a seaplane-handling derrick added aft of it. A Curtiss SOC floatplane is perched on what was the flight deck. *National Archives*

Martin MS.1 aboard *S1* at Hampton Roads, 24 October 1923. The cylindrical hangar is prominent aft of the conning tower. *Author's collection*

Select Bibliography

Bruce, J M, *British Aeroplanes 1914–1918*, Putnam, London, 1957

Dittmar, F J, and College, J J, *British Warships 1914–1919*, Ian Allan, London, 1972

Dousset, Francis, *Les porte-avions français*, Editions de la Cité, Brest, 1978

Fraccaroli, Aldo, *Italian Warships of World War I*, Ian Allan, London, 1970

Greger, René, *Die russische Flotte im ersten Weltkrieg*, J F Lehmanns, Munich, 1970

Greger, René, *Austro-Hungarian Warships of World War I*, Ian Allen, London, 1976

Jung, Dieter, Wenzel, Berndt, and Abendroth, Arno, *Die Schiffe und Boote der deutschen Seeflieger*, Motorbuch, Stuttgart, 1977

Kohri, Katsu, Komori, Ikuo, and Naito, Ichiro, *The Fifty Years of Japanese Aviation 1910-1960*, 3 vols. Kantosha, Tokyo, 1960-61

Layman, R D, *To Ascend From a Floating Base*, Fairleigh Dickinson University Press, Cranbury, N J, and Associated University Presses, London, 1979

Nowarra, Heinz, Robertson, Bruce, and Cooksley, Peter G, *Marine Aircraft of the 1914-1918 War*, Harleyford, Letchworth, 1966

Pavlovich, N B, ed. *Flot v pervoi mirovoi voine*, 2 vols, Ministry of Defence, Moscow, 1964

Raleigh, Walter, and Jones, H A, *The War in the Air*, 6 vols, Oxford University Press, London, 1922-37

Roskill, B W, ed. *Documents Relating to the Naval Air Service*, vol 1, Naval Records Society, London, 1969

Turnbull, Archibald D, and Lord, Clifford L, *History of United States Naval Aviation*, Yale University Press, New Haven, 1949

US Navy Department, *Dictionary of Amercian Naval Fighting Ships*, 8 vols, Government Printing Office, Washington, 1959-81

Van Deurs, George, *Wings for the Fleet*, US Naval Institute, Annapolis, 1966

INDEX

Page numbers in Italic indicate illustrations